COASTERS OF THE KIEL CANAL

KÜMOS DES NORD-OSTSEE-KANALS

by Bernard McCall and Oliver Sesemann

INTRODUCTION

This, the second book in the *Coasters of ...* series, is our first venture into a bi-lingual publication. *Coasters of the Kiel Canal* takes a geographic approach and the reader will follow along the canal from Brunsbüttel in the west to Kiel at the Baltic end of the busiest artificial waterway in the world.

Due to the geography of the region, northern Europe and Scandinavia have always been linked by ships and thus the Kiel Canal, originally planned as a military waterway, provided international merchant shipping with a valuable short cut to/from the Baltic Sea and shelter from fierce storms around the Skaw. Among the 42,000 ships which pass the canal annually (2004), it is coastal shipping in particular which depends on the canal - but on which the canal relies, too. Hence the Kiel Canal has been promoted by the EU as part of their TEN programme to help ease congestion on the roads.

As a consequence of its importance, the canal has mirrored shipping's structural changes since its opening in 1895. From the 1960s onwards, this was represented, firstly, by the change from the traditional coaster to more unitised ship types (e.g. container and ro/ro vessels, ships for palletised cargoes) and, secondly, in the following years by a continuing specialisation of these. And although the combination of the region's geography and the survival of the German captain/owner structure of ship owning has saved many traditionally shaped coasters from the blast furnaces, coastal shipping has, thirdly, become more international and capital intensive with larger fleets, bigger vessels and different ownership structures. Furthermore, while reflecting all these changes, shortsea traders have become integral parts of the cultural landscape as well; they belong to the canal, perhaps more than many a deepsea vessel with only occasional appearances.

This book is to reflect modern coastal shipping as a product of the above developments. Hence, the photographs show a selection of coasters in their familiar environment of the Kiel Canal today. Nevertheless, there is also a number of flashbacks with ships which have long left this part of the world; these scenes serve to emphasize the ongoing process coastal shipping on the canal is part of. Despite all considerations, however, a book like this can never claim to be fully comprehensive. We acknowledge the help of Gil Mayes in checking early drafts of this book.

Der vorliegende Bildband ist der zweite in der „Coasters of ..." -Reihe und gleichzeitig unsere erste zweisprachige Veröffentlichung. Dem geographischen Grundkonzept der Reihe folgend nimmt „Coasters of the Kiel Canal" den Leser mit auf eine Reise von Brunsbüttel bis nach Kiel, immer entlang der meistbefahrenen künstlichen Wasserstraße der Welt.

Die Lage Skandinaviens zu Nordeuropa hat schon immer den Waren- und Personentransport per Schiff gefördert. Die internationale Handelsschifffahrt erkannte dann auch schnell den schützenden und wegverkürzenden Wert des 1895 eröffneten Nord-Ostsee-Kanals (NOK), der zunächst lediglich als militärstrategische Wasserstraße geplant worden war. Von den heute rund 42.000 Schiffen, die den Kanal jährlich nutzen (2004), stützt sich insbesondere die Küstenschifffahrt auf diese Vorteile und sichert gleichzeitig seine Grundauslastung. Die Bedeutung des NOK wird ferner unterstrichen durch die Aufnahme in das TEN-Förderprogramm der EU zur Entlastung der europäischen Fernstraßen.

Durch seine zentrale Rolle in den Ostseeverkehren war der NOK seit jeher Projektionsfläche des ständigen Wandels. Insbesondere seit den 1960er Jahren lassen sich hier drei Entwicklungsschritte ablesen: Zunächst wurde das traditionelle Küstenmotorschiff immer mehr durch auf Einheitsladungen spezialisierte Schiffstypen (u.a. Container-, Ro/Ro-Schiffe, Palettencarrier) heraus. Obwohl eine beachtliche Anzahl an „richtigen" Kümos wegen der kleinräumigen Fahrtgebiete und der althergebrachten Eigentumsverhältnisse in der deutschen Küstenfahrt (Kapitän-Eigner-Struktur) noch bis heute hier im Einsatz ist, sind Internationalisierung und Industrialisierung des Geschäfts deutlich als dritter Entwicklungsschritt zu beobachten. Indikatoren sind u.a. größere Flotten, zunehmende Schiffsgrößen sowie völlig neue Reedereistrukturen. Während also die Kümos des NOK zum Einen für eine Entwicklungsdynamik stehen, sind sie zum Anderen doch zu einem festen Bestandteil der Kulturlandschaft Nord-Ostsee-Kanal geworden. Dies gilt insbesondere im Gegensatz zu vielen Frachtern der großen Fahrt, deren weltweite Routen nicht ganz so oft durch Schleswig-Holstein führen.

Das vorliegende Buch soll das gegenwärtige Bild der Küstenschifffahrt auf dem NOK repräsentieren, das als Ergebnis der oben beschriebenen Entwicklung zu sehen ist. Folglich zeigen die Fotos eine Auswahl typischer Alltagsszenen der jüngeren Vergangenheit; der eine oder andere Rückblick soll dabei an den steten Wandel erinnern. Trotz gründlicher Abwägungen kann ein Projekt wie dieses jedoch niemals den Anspruch auf Vollständigkeit erheben. Wir möchten an dieser Stelle Gil Mayes für die Unterstützung in der Frühphase des Buches danken.

Bernard McCall
Portishead, England

Oliver Sesemann
Kiel, Deutschland

July 2005

Published by Bernard McCall, 400 Nore Road, Portishead, Bristol, BS20 8EZ, England. Website : www.coastalshipping.co.uk
Telephone/fax : 01275 846178. E-mail : bernard@coastalshipping.co.uk
All distribution enquiries should be addressed to the publisher.

Printed by Amadeus Press, Ezra House, West 26 Business Park, Cleckheaton, West Yorkshire, BD19 4TQ
Telephone : 01274 863210; fax : 01274 863211; e-mail : info@amadeuspress.co.uk; website : www.amadeuspress.co.uk

ISBN : 1-902953-18-5

Front cover : With the houses of Holtenau in the backgound, the immaculate **Kaja-H** *(DEU, 492gt/55) begins a westward passage along the canal during a voyage from Heiligenhafen to Hamburg on 1 August 1991.*

Das bekannte Häuserensemble Kiel-Holtenaus passierend verlässt die gepflegte **Kaja-H** *(DEU, 492 BRZ/55) am 1. August 1991 die Schleusen auf dem Weg von Heiligenhafen nach Hamburg.* (Bernard McCall)

Back cover : Shortly after passing the attractive canalside village of Sehestedt, the **Wilhelmine Steffens** *(DEU, 1156gt/81), bound from Helsingborg to Goole with a cargo of phosphates, approaches the large Audorf/Rade siding on the cold afternoon of 29 December 2004.*

Kurz nachdem sie Sehestedt durchfahren hat, biegt die **Wilhelmine Steffens** *(DEU, 1156 BRZ/81) am späten Nachmittag des kalten 29. Dezember 2004 in die Großweiche Rade/Audorf ein. Sie ist mit Phosphaten auf der Reise von Helsingborg nach Goole.* (Oliver Sesemann)

The Kiel Canal

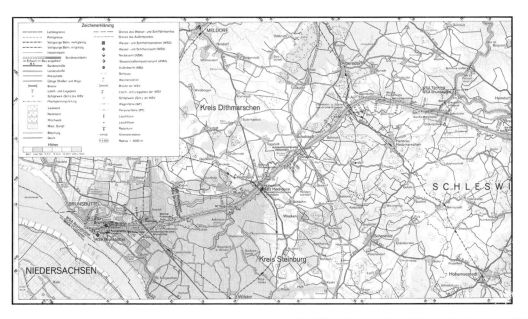

We begin our journey at Brunsbüttel and photographed leaving the southern pair of locks, known as the Alte Schleusen (Old Locks) on 16 January 2005 is the *Osteborg* (ANT, 1999gt/92), ex *Zeus*-99. In the background is the Brunsbüttel VTS office. The coaster is part of the fleet of the Dutch Wagenborg shipping company whose ships frequently use the Kiel Canal on their extensive network of coastal routes as well as on their services between Scandinavia and North America. Like most of the Wagenborg vessels, the *Osteborg* is Dutch-built, having been delivered by the Bijlsma shipyard in Wartena.

Zu Beginn unserer Reise durch den Nord-Ostsee-Kanal verlässt die *Osteborg* (ANT, 1999 BRZ/92), ex *Zeus*-99, am 16. Januar 2005 die alte Nordschleuse in Brunsbüttel in Richtung Elbe. Im Hintergrund ist die Verkehrszentrale auf der Schleuseninsel zu sehen. *Osteborg* gehört zu der niederländischen Koninklijke Wagenborg Reederei, deren Schiffe sowohl in der europäischen Küstenfahrt als auch auf Transatlantikdiensten eingesetzt werden und auf ihren Reisen häufig den Nord-Ostsee-Kanal passieren. Die meisten Wagenborg-Schiffe wurden in den Niederlanden gebaut, die *Osteborg* bei Bijlsma in Wartena.

(Oliver Sesemann)

The northern pair of locks are the Neue Schleusen (New Locks) and the **Patriot** (CYP, 2163gt/94) makes her approach as she heads westbound on the morning of 28 July 1996. Built at the Hugo Peters shipyard in Wewelsfleth, this coaster is operated by Interscan and is specially equipped for work in the paper trade. For this, she is fitted with a side loading ramp and 15-tonne lift. She usually loads reels of paper in Finnish ports such as Hamina for delivery to the UK and the Iberian peninsula.

Am Ende einer westgehenden Passage am 28. Juli 1996 läuft die **Patriot** (CYP, 2163 BRZ/94) die neuen Schleusen an. Sie wurde bei der Hugo Peters Schiffswerft in Wewelsfleth gebaut und ist mit ihrem seitlichen Tor, hinter dem sich ein 15-Tonnen-Lift verbirgt, speziell für den Papiertransport ihres Charterers Interscan ausgerüstet. **Patriot** ist auf einer regelmäßigen Route eingesetzt und lädt Papierrollen in finnischen Häfen wie Hamina, um sie nach Großbritannien und Spanien/Portugal zu bringen.

(Bernard McCall)

Many of the ships featured in this book were built at shipyards along the canal or along the River Elbe. The veteran *Elvi Kull* (ATG, 474gt/55), ex *Jens Peter*-84, *Reinhold Krusemark*-62, makes for the old locks at Brunsbüttel at the end of a westbound passage along the canal on 28 July 1996. This coaster, lengthened in 1958 and again in 1978, was built at the Nobiskrug shipyard in Rendsburg and continues to be seen regularly on the canal.

Eine ganze Reihe von Schiffen in diesem Band wurde von Werften am Nord-Ostsee-Kanal erbaut. Die betagte *Elvi Kull* (ATG, 474 BRZ/55), ex *Jens Peter*-84, *Reinhold Krusemark*-62, läuft hier gerade die alten Schleusen an, ebenfalls nach einer westwärtigen Passage am 28. Juli 1996. Dieses Kümo wurde auf der Werft Nobiskrug in Rendsburg erbaut und in den Jahren 1958 und 1978 verlängert. *Elvi Kull* ist ein treuer Kunde der Wasserstraße.

(Bernard McCall)

he **Henny** (GBR, 2966gt/97) leaves the Neue Schleusen and begins an eastbound passage ong the canal on 1 June 2004. She is working on a route linking Bremerhaven and Hamburg to ödertälje and Västerås in Sweden. She was built at the Kröger Werft yard at Schacht-Audorf on e outskirts of Rendsburg. Originally flying the German flag, she has now transferred to the ritish flag which allows her to sail with one engineer rather than the two required by German les.

Am 1. Juni 2004 verlässt die **Henny** (GBR, 2966 BRZ/97) die neuen Schleusen auf dem Weg von Bremerhaven und Hamburg nach Södertalje und Västerås in Schweden. Ursprünglich fuhr das bei der Kröger-Werft in Schacht-Audorf bei Rendsburg gebaute Schiff unter der deutschen Flagge. Hier jedoch weht bereits die britische Flagge am Heck, da ihr Reeder so nur einen statt zwei Ingenieure einsetzen muss.

(Bernard McCall)

The skies are threatening on the morning of 28 July 1996 as the **Buxtehude** (CYP, 2565gt/85), recently renamed from **Rita**, gets under way after a brief stop at the southern quays at Brunsbüttel. She is a product of the J J Sietas yard at Neuenfelde on the outskirts of Hamburg and belongs to the yard's type 130/130c.

Ein Sommergewitter liegt in der Luft, als die **Buxtehude** (CYP, 2565 BRZ/85), ex **Rita**-95, kurz nach ihrer Umbenennung, am 28. Juli 1996 die Brunsbütteler Südkaje verlässt. Sie ist ein Produkt der Werft J. J. Sietas in Neuenfelde bei Hamburg und gehört zu dem 13 Einheiten umfassenden Werfttyp 130/130c.

(Bernard McCall)

Approaching the South Quay on 5 February 2005 is the coaster **Suntis** (DEU, 1564gt/85). Together with fleetmate **Montis**, this ship is owned in Itzehoe, a medium-sized town south of Brunsbüttel. She belongs to a large series of 39 similar coasters built in the mid-1980s by the Hugo Peters shipyard at Wewelsfleth, also a few kilometres south of Brunsbüttel. The ship is employed on routes linking Scandinavian ports with ports in northwest Europe and the UK.

Am 5. Februar 2005 läuft die **Suntis** (DEU, 1564 BRZ/85) den Südkai an. Sie und ihr Schwesterschiff **Montis** sind in Itzehoe beheimatet, das ein paar Kilometer südlich von Brunsbüttel liegt. Auch wurden beide einige Kilometer südlich von Brunsbüttel gebaut, nämlich in Wewelsfleth bei der Hugo Peters-Werft als Teil einer ganzen Serie von 39 ähnlichen rheingängigen Einheiten. **Suntis** befährt den Kanal regelmäßig auf ihren Reisen zwischen Skandinavien und nordwesteuropäischen und englischen Häfen.

(Oliver Sesemann)

Our final view of the southern quays shows the *Susann* (ATG, 526gt/39), ex *Ruth*-89, *Hans Georg*-89, *Morild*-65, *Sigborg*-58, *Reze*-40, awaiting orders on 28 July 1996. This veteran coaster was built at the yard of A Vuyk & Zonen at Capelle a/d IJssel. She continued to trade in northern Germany and the Baltic until 2001 when she was bought by Caribbean owners and renamed *La Family Island Express*.

Ein letzter Blick auf die Südkaje zeigt die *Susann* (ATG, 526 BRZ/39), ex *Ruth*-89, *Hans-Georg*-89, *Morild*-65, *Sigborg*-58, *Reze*-40, die hier am 28. Juli 1996 die nächste Order erwartet. Dieser Veteran wurde bei der Werft A Vuyk & Zonen in Capelle a/d IJssel erbaut. Bis zum Jahre 2001 war das Schiff regelmäßig auf dem Kanal unterwegs, danach ging es an neue Eigner in der Karibik und wurde in *La Family Island Express* umbenannt.

(Bernard McCall)

On the northern side of the canal, opposite the berth occupied by the **Susann**, are other lay-by berths. It was at one such berth that the **Elisabeth** (DEU, 1139gt/83) was photographed early on the morning of 10 August 2002 when on passage to Southampton. This attractive coaster is owned in Husum, and it was at the local Husumer Schiffswerft that she was built. Also at this point are berths for a wide variety of workboats owned by the canal authority such as the dredger **Wilhelm Krüger**..

Auf der gegenüber liegenden Seite des Kanals befinden sich ebenfalls einige Anleger, z.T. mit Bunkermöglichkeit. Eine von ihnen ist am 10. August 2002 von der **Elisabeth** (DEU, 1139 BRZ/83) belegt, die hier kurz ihre Reise nach Southampton unterbricht. Dieses attraktive kleine Schiff ist in Husum beheimatet, wo es auch von der Husumer Schiffswerft gebaut wurde. Im Hintergrund ist der Saugbagger **Wilhelm Krüger** zu erkennen, der im Betriebshafen auf seinen nächsten Einsatz zum Freibaggern der Schleusenzufahrt wartet.

(Jim McFaul)

A considerable number of ships using the canal are feeder vessels carrying containers to and from Hamburg, Bremerhaven and occasionally other ports south of the Elbe. Many of these are operated by two major companies, Team Lines and UniFeeder. The **Anke Ehler** (DEU, 5067gt/00), built by J J Sietas, was working for Århus-based UniFeeder on a service linking Felixstowe and Rotterdam to Gothenburg, Helsingborg and Copenhagen when photographed heading west on 5 August 2003. She is registered in Otterndorf, a small town near Cuxhaven. In the background one of the small cross-canal ferries can be seen heading for Ostermoor, a little over 4 km east of Brunsbüttel.

Eine nicht geringe Anzahl der Schiffe, die regelmäßig den NOK befahren sind Containerfeeder, die die nordwesteuropäischen Seehäfen mit dem Ostseeraum verbinden. Viele von ihnen werden durch die beiden Hauptcharterer auf diesem Gebiet, Team Lines und UniFeeder betrieben. Die **Anke Ehler** (DEU, 5067 BRZ/00), gebaut bei J. J. Sietas, fährt hier am 5. August 2003 für die in Århus ansässige UniFeeder auf einer Route zwischen Felixstowe, Rotterdam, Göteborg, Helsingborg und Kopenhagen. Im Hintergrund kreuzt die Fähre Ostermoor den Kanal, etwa vier Kilometer östlich von Brunsbüttel, nahe der Hochbrücke mit der B5.

(Bernard McCall)

On the southern bank of the canal at this point are bunkering berths. On 1 June 2004, the *Giessenborg* (ANT, 2820gt/97), ex *Baltic Erin*-03, *Giessenborg*-99, was taking on bunker fuel at the No. 3 berth and the *Bärbel P* (GIB, 2301gt/00) at the No. 1 berth. Both ships were built on the Winschoterdiep in northern Holland, the *Giessenborg* at the Bodewes shipyard in Hoogezand, and the *Bärbel P* at the Pattje yard in Waterhuizen although her hull had been built in Mangalia by Daewoo-Mangalia Heavy Industries and had been launched as *Heinrich G*.

Am südlichen Ufer des Kanals zwischen Brunsbüttel und Ostermoor liegen Bunkerplätze, wo am 1. Juni 2004 die *Giessenborg* (ANT, 2820 BRZ/97), ex *Baltic Erin*-03, *Giessenborg*-99, Jetty Nr. 3 belegt, während die *Bärbel P* (GIB, 2301 BRZ/00) an Nr. 1 liegt. Beide Schiffe wurden am Winschoterdiep in den Niederlanden gebaut, *Giessenborg* bei der Bodewes-Werft in Hoogezand, *Bärbel P* als *Heinrich G* bei der Pattje-Werft in Waterhuizen, nachdem der Rumpf von Daewoo-Mangalia Heavy Industries am Schwarzen Meer zugeliefert wurde.

(Bernard McCall)

7,5 km east of Brunsbüttel is the small ferry crossing at Kudensee. This is the location for the photograph of the **Volgoneft 251** (RUS, 3463gt/75) leading a line of other eastbound vessels on 30 May 1995. This tanker was built at the Volgogradskiy Sudostroitelnyy Zavod shipyard and is one of many used mainly to carry oil along the Russian waterway system from the Caspian Sea to ports in the west. The bridge in the background, visible also in the photograph on page 12, carries the B5 road north-west from Hamburg towards Husum.

7,5 Kilometer östlich von Brunsbüttel liegt der kleine Ort Kudensee, wo auch eine Fähre die Wasserstraße quert. Am 30. Mai 1995 läuft hier die ostgehende **Volgoneft 251** (RUS, 3463 BRZ/75) als erstes von mehreren Schiffen aus einer Schleusenkammer auf die Fährstelle zu. Im Hintergrund ist die Hochbrücke bei Ostermoor zu erkennen. Der Tanker ist eines der vielen russischen Fluss-/Seeschiffe, die regelmäßig den Kanal passieren. Gebaut bei der Werft Sudostroitelnyy Zavod in Wolgograd, sind diese Schiffe für den Verkehr auf dem weitverzweigten russischen Fluss- und Kanalsystem geeignet und können gleichzeitig Strecken über See bewältigen.

(Bernard McCall)

14

The stretch of the canal between the Ostermoor ferry and Hochdonn is remarkable because the surrounding land lies below the water level in this part. It is here, between Kudensee and Burg ferries, that we see the **Comet** (DEU, 3999gt/98) heading west on 16 January 2005. Typical of today's smaller container feeder, the vessel was built by the J J Sietas shipyard in Neuenfelde near Hamburg as part of the Type 151 series of 23 nearly-identical sister ships.

Zwischen Ostermoor und Hochdonn führt der Kanal eingedeicht durch Marschlandschaft, die unter dem Kanalwasserspiegel liegt. Innerhalb dieses Abschnitts, zwischen Burg und Kudensee, ist hier am 16. Januar 2005 die **Comet** (DEU, 3999 BRZ/98) unterwegs nach Brunsbüttel. Das Schiff ist ein typisches Beispiel für die kleineren Containerfeeder in den Ostseeverkehren. Sie wurde von der Werft J. J. Sietas als Teil einer Serie von 23 Schiffen des Typs 151 gebaut.

(Oliver Sesemann)

At the 16 km point is the next small ferry crossing, named Burg after the small town located on the northern side of the canal. As new ferries have been brought into use over the years, so have their landing stages and ramps been upgraded. As a result, previous ramps are visible and make excellent vantage points. There are also parking areas at many of these locations and these as well as the "Burger Fährhaus" restaurant nearby are very popular in the summer months. Passing the ferry berthed on the northern side of the canal on 1 June 2004 is the *Hege* (NIS, 3004gt/75), ex *Koningshaven*-01, *OPDR Rabat*-98, *Rabat*-97, *Diana II*-88, *Diana*-83. This ship was built by J J Sietas.

Bei Kanalkilometer 16 liegt die Fährstelle Burg. Nachdem die Querverkehre den heutigen Erfordernissen angepasst wurden, bieten die alten Fähranlagen sehr gute Aussichtsmöglichkeiten, die wegen der nahen Parkplätze im Sommer hoch frequentiert sind. Am 1. Juni 2004 passiert die *Hege* (NIS, 3004 BRZ/75), ex *Koningshaven*-01, *OPDR Rabat*-98, *Rabat*-97, *Diana II*-88, *Diana*-83, die Fähre Burg, nahe deren nördlichem Anleger das beliebte Ausflugslokal „Burger Fährhaus" liegt.

(Bernard McCall)

There is no doubt that roll on/roll off vessels have replaced conventional coasters in many trades but they have a legitimate place in books such as this for they will be the "coasters" of future generations. A typical example is the **Trans Botnia** (NIS, 12076gt/99) which was on passage from Antwerp to the Finnish port of Hamina, her customary route. The ship's hull was built at the Damen subsidiary yard in Galati and was completed by Fosen Mek Verksteder at Rissa. She was photographed as she passed beneath the high level rail bridge (Eisenbahnhochbrücke) at Hochdonn on 31 July 2002. The railway line is that linking Hamburg to Husum and Westerland, and rail enthusiasts will note the passenger train crossing the bridge and heading for Hamburg, hauled by a diesel hydraulic locomotive.

Zweifelsohne haben moderne RoRo-Schiffe mit der Zeit immer mehr Ladung aus der traditionellen Küstenschifffahrt übernommen, auch weil heute viel Ladung per Trailer transportiert wird. Daher müssen solche Schiffe als „Kümos der Zukunft" bezeichnet werden. Ein typisches Exemplar ist die **Trans Botnia** (NIS, 12076 BRZ/99), die hier am 31. Juli 2002 auf ihrer regelmäßigen Rundreise von Antwerpen nach Hamina in Finnland Hochdonn passiert. Das Schiff wurde bei Fosen Mek Verksteder in Rissa, Norwegen, erbaut, wobei der Rumpf von der rumänischen Tochter der niederländischen Damen Werft in Galati zugeliefert wurde. Die Eisenbahnhochbrücke, die hier bei Hochdonn den Kanal quert, trägt die sogenannte Marschbahn. Eine Diesellok zieht hier gerade einen Zug in südlicher Richtung über das Bauwerk.

(Dominic McCall)

On the same date as the previous photograph, the **Oraness** (DIS, 1850gt/85) was photographed as she headed eastwards past Hochdonn. This interesting vessel was built at the Tille shipyard in Kootstertille as a dry cargo ship named **Elisa von Barssel**. Soon renamed **Flagship I** she became **Lia Ventura** in 1986 and then **Inisheer** in 1988 following acquisition by Arklow Shipping. Between 1995 and 1999 she was renamed **Dunkerque Express** and was sold out of the Arklow fleet in 2002. Acquired by Danish tanker operator M H Simonsen, she was converted to a tanker and renamed **Oraness**.

Am selben Tag passiert auch die **Oraness** (DIS, 1850 BRZ/85) Hochdonn. Dieses Schiff hat eine interessante Geschichte. Gebaut wurde es auf der Tille Werft in Kootstertille in den Niederlanden als Trockenfrachter **Elisa von Barssel**, fuhr dann als **Flagship** I-86 und **Lia Ventura**-88, bevor es an Arklow Shipping verkauft und in **Inisheer** umbenannt wurde. Zwischen 1995 und 1999 trug es für dieselben Eigner den Namen **Dunkerque Express**. Nach seinem Verkauf an die dänische Tankerreederei M H Simonsen im Jahre 2002 schließlich wurde das Schiff in einen Tanker umgebaut und bekam seinen heutigen Namen.

(Dominic McCall)

The Kiel Canal leads through the very rural landscape of Schleswig-Holstein with many farms nearby. Consequently, there a number of grain silos and small wharves directly on the canal banks, such as this at Hochdonn. A third vessel noted at Hochdonn on 31 July 2002 was the container feeder ship **Betsy** (DEU, 2988gt/98), on charter to Team Lines, which was heading west on her usual route from Gdynia to Hamburg and Bremerhaven. The hull of the ship was built at the Societatea Comerciala Navol yard in Oltenita and the ship was completed at the Kröger Werft yard in Schacht-Audorf. The cross-canal ferry is seen at the right of the photograph.

Der Nord-Ostsee-Kanal durchquert eine wesentlich von der Landwirtschaft geprägte Region. Oft reichen die Felder bis direkt an die Wasserstraße heran. Daher existieren auch einige Verladestellen direkt am Kanal, wie diese hier in Hochdonn, wo sich auch eine Fährstelle befindet. Am 31. Juli 2002 passiert hier der Containerfeeder **Betsy** (DEU, 2988 BRZ/98) auf ihrer Rundreise von Gdynia nach Hamburg und Bremerhaven im Rahmen einer Team-Lines-Charter. Der Rumpf dieses Schiffes wurde von der Werft Societatea Comerciala Navol in Oltenita gefertigt, um dann bei der Kröger-Werft in Schacht-Audorf ausgerüstet zu werden.

(Dominic McCall)

Having just berthed at Hohenhörn, the crew of the coaster *Hammelwarden* (DEU, 388gt/60) are tightening the ropes while the *Alblas* (NLD, 3443gt/96) is sailing past on her way to the Baltic on 23 January 2005. The vehicle ferry and motorway bridge crossing the canal in this place can be seen in the background. The *Hammelwarden* was built by C. Lühring Schiffswerft in Brake on the River Weser and lengthened no fewer than three times (1968, 1972, 1978). The *Alblas* was built by Severnav SA in Turnu Severin, Bulgaria.

Am 23. Januar 2005 hat gerade der kleine Frachter *Hammelwarden* (DEU, 388 BRZ/60) am Silo in Hohenhörn festgemacht. Die zweiköpfige Mannschaft hat kein Auge für die niederländische *Alblas* (NLD, 3443 BRZ/96), die auf ihrem Weg in die Ostsee an dieser Stelle die Fährlinie kreuzt. Im Hintergrund ist die Autobahnhochbrücke Schafstedt zu sehen, die die A 23 über den Kanal führt. *Hammelwarden* wurde in Brake/Weser bei der Schiffswerft C. Lühring gebaut und bisher insgesamt dreimal (1968, 1972, 1978) verlängert. *Alblas* ist ein Produkt der Werft Severnav SA im bulgarischen Turnu Severin.

(Oliver Sesemann)

Another Sietas-built coaster, the **Hydra** (CYP, 1545gt/79), ex **Waalborg**-93, **Vera Rambow**-89, passes the siding at Dükerswisch on 21 July 1995 with a full cargo of timber. This siding is situated 22 km from Brunsbüttel and is one of twelve along the canal, allowing vessels to wait for others to pass. This is often necessary when one vessel is large or is carrying dangerous cargo. Sawn timber is not such a dangerous cargo! The coaster was later renamed **Elm** and presently sails for Polish owners as **Rega**,

Ein weiteres von J.J. Sietas erbautes Schiff ist die **Hydra** (CYP, 1545 BRZ/79), ex **Waalborg**-93, **Vera Rambow**-89, die hier am 21. Juli 1995 die Weiche Dükerswisch, ca. 22 Kilometer östlich von Brunsbüttel, passiert. Es bestehen insgesamt zwölf Ausweichstellen, sogenannte Weichen, am Kanal. An diesen Stellen können sich auch größere Schiffe oder Schiffe mit gefährlicher Ladung begegnen, die sich nach den Vorgaben des Verkehrsgruppensystems auf Strecke nicht begegnen könnten oder dürften. Mit Schnittholz hat die **Hydra** jedoch keine gefährliche Ladung an Bord. Das Schiff wurde später in **Elm** umbenannt und fährt inzwischen für polnische Eigner als **Rega**.

(Bernard McCall)

Forest products and trailer transportation between Scandinavia and the Continent have always played a vital part in shipping on the canal. As mentioned on page 18, the ro/ro vessels employed in these trades must be considered as modern-day coasters. One of the earliest examples of this specialised type of vessel is the **Blue Sky** (NIS, 5086gt/74), ex **Flipper**-94, **Monaco**-86, **Tuulia**-85, **Iggesund**-81. In this view she sails along near Grünental between Dükerswisch and Fischerhütte sidings on a tranquil, sunny 10 June 1996. **Blue Sky** was built as part of a trio at the Lindenau shipyard in Kiel. All three ships have since left the Baltic trades, replaced by much larger tonnage.

Rollende Ladung zwischen Skandinavien und Nordwesteuropa besteht sowohl aus Trailern als auch aus besonders verstauten Forstprodukten wie Papier. Sie wird von speziell entwickelten RoRo-Schiffen transportiert, die in diesem Teil der Welt als moderne Küstenmotorschiffe gelten müssen. Ein frühes Exemplar ist die **Blue Sky** (NIS, 5086 BRZ/74), ex **Flipper**-94, **Monaco**-86, **Tuulia**-85, **Iggesund**-81, die hier am 10. Juni 1996 zwischen den Weichen Dükerswisch und Fischerhütte Grünental passiert. **Blue Sky** ist Teil eines Trios, das auf der Lindenau Werft in Kiel-Friedrichsort entstand. Inzwischen haben alle drei Schiffe die Ostseedienste verlassen, ersetzt durch wesentlich größere Tonnage.

(Oliver Sesemann)

It is the same location but seen from the opposite bank of the canal when the chemical tanker *Vivaldi* (NIS, 3922gt/82), ex *Echoman*-97, makes her way towards Brunsbüttel on the sunny morning of 22 January 2005. The ship was built by Appledore Shipbuilders Ltd. The bridge at Grünental, completed in 1986, is a replacement of the original crossing (built in 1892) which had to be removed in the course of canal extension works that started in 1965 and reached this place in the 1980s. The old bridge was identical to the one that still exists at Levensau.

Selber Ort, andere Perspektive: Der von Appledore Shipbuilders Ltd. im englischen Appledore gebaute Chemietanker *Vivaldi* (NIS, 3922 BRZ/82), ex *Echoman*-97, pflügt am 22. Januar 2005 durch die Geest bei Albersdorf und passiert dabei die Grünentaler Hochbrücke. Diese wurde 1986 fertig gestellt als Ersatz für die ursprüngliche Brücke von 1892, die der Erweiterung des Kanalbettes, die ab 1965 statt fand und diesen Ort in den 1980er Jahren erreichte, im Wege stand. Die Brücke war baugleich mit der noch existierenden alten Levensauer Hochbrücke.

(Oliver Sesemann)

At the eastern end of the Fischerhütte siding another vehicle ferry crosses the canal. It is at this point that the eastbound Estonian-owned coaster **Erlanda** (VCT, 1999gt/91), ex **Scheldeborg**-04, passes the westbound German-owned ro/ro vessel **Scan Hansa** (IOM, 8821gt/99) on a cold 22 January 2005. Built at the Bijlsma Wartena shipyard, the coaster is a sister ship of the **Osteborg** which can be seen on page 4.

Am Ostende der Weiche Fischerhütte quert eine weitere Fähre die Wasserstraße. An dieser Stelle begegnen wo sich am 22. Januar 2005 die ostwärts fahrende estnische **Erlanda** (VCT, 1999 BRZ/91), ex **Scheldeborg**-04, und die deutsche **Scan Hansa** (IOM, 8821 BRZ/99). **Erlanda** ist ein Schwesterschiff der **Osteborg** (vgl. S. 4), wurde also von der Bijlsma Wartena-Werft erbaut.

(Oliver Sesemann)

Only five kilometres east of Fischerhütte siding and ferry, at the 40 kilometre point, are Oldenbüttel siding and ferry. Here, we see the general cargo ship ***Bremer Anna*** (GIB, 3152gt/03) sailing past the ferry landing, also on 22 January 2005. The ship is owned by Reederei Rörd Braren, of Kollmar on the river Elbe, who are renowned for their environmentally friendly ships. All four vessels of the fleet are employed in the forest products trade, mainly between Scandinavia and northwest Europe, and can therefore be seen on the canal quite frequently. While three of Braren's ships have been built by the Hugo Peters shipyard at Wewelsfleth, ***Bremer Anna*** was completed by Bodewes Scheepswerfen B.V., of Hoogezand-Martenshoek. Her hull was built at a Polish shipyard.

Nur fünf Kilometer weiter östlich liegt bei Kanalkilometer 40 der kleine Ort Oldenbüttel. Ebenfalls am 22. Januar 2005 passiert die westgehende ***Bremer Anna*** (GIB, 3152 BRZ/03) die dortige Fährstelle. Reeder Rörd Braren aus Kollmar an der Elbe ist inzwischen sehr bekannt für die Umweltfreundlichkeit seiner Schiffe, die auch entsprechende Auszeichnungen tragen. Alle vier Flottenmitglieder werden hauptsächlich im Forstproduktenverkehr zwischen Skandinavien und Nordwesteuropa eingesetzt, weswegen sie häufig auch im Nord-Ostsee-Kanal anzutreffen sind. Drei seiner Schiffe ließ Braren bei der Hugo Peters Schiffswerft in Wewelsfleth, quasi in direkter Nachbarschaft zu deren Heimathafen, bauen. Die ***Bremer Anna*** allerdings wurde von der Bodewes Scheepswerfen B.V. in Hoogezand-Martenshoek erbaut, nachdem der Rumpf aus Polen zugeliefert wurde.

(Oliver Sesemann)

On the same sunny day, the **Lore Prahm** (DEU, 1156gt/89) also passes Oldenbüttel en route to Brunsbüttel. The road signs indicate that onlookers can get close to the waterway, and indeed tourism around the canal region is thriving. The ship's deck cargo of sawn timber, being carried from Karlshamn to the Channel Islands, is a typical example of the Baltic's coastal shipping outside the container feeder trades. Built at the Gebr. Kötter shipyard in Haren on the River Ems, **Lore Prahm** belongs to the eight-strong fleet of Hammann & Prahm Reederei of Wischhafen.

Am selben Tag passiert das Frachtschiff **Lore Prahm** (DEU, 1156 BRZ/89) Oldenbüttel auf dem Weg nach Brunsbüttel. Die Straßenschilder machen die Attraktivität der Kanalumgebung deutlich, die den Tourismus als wichtigen Wirtschaftsfaktor dieser ländlichen Region fördert. Die Decksladung Holz ist charakteristisch für den Seehandel der Ostseeregion, von den dominierenden Containerverkehren einmal abgesehen. Die **Lore Prahm** wurde von der Gebr. Kötter Werft in Haren/Ems erbaut und ist eines von acht Schiffen der Hammann & Prahm Reederei aus Wischhafen/Elbe. Das Schiff befindet sich auf der Reise von Karlshamn in Schweden zu nach den Kanalinseln.

(Oliver Sesemann)

The siding at Breiholz is 48,5 km from Brunsbüttel. Passing this point on a westbound voyage on 5 August 2003 is the *Yuko* (ANT, 920gt/86). Built at the Ferus Smit yard in Westerbroek as *Laura*, she became *Sayonara* in 1993 and then *Hera* and *Noordzee* in quick succession in 1999. She had taken the name *Yuko* in mid-March 2003.

Auf der Hälfte der Strecke bei Kilometer 48,5 befindet sich die Weiche Breiholz. Am 5. August 2003 passiert die westgehende *Yuko* (ANT, 920 BRZ/86) diese Stelle, an deren östlichen Ausgang eine weitere Fähre den Kanal kreuzt. *Yuko* wurde als *Laura*-93 bei Ferus Smit im niederländischen Westerbroek gebaut. Nachdem sie bis 1999 als *Sayonara* fuhr, wechselte sie in diesem Jahr den Namen zweimal, nämlich in *Hera* und *Noordzee*, bevor sie schließlich Mitte März 2003 ihren heutigen Namen erhielt.

(Bernard McCall)

Situated exactly at the 50 km mark is the ferry crossing at Breiholz. Passing this location and heading west on 23 July 2002 is the *Tonja* (HND, 498gt/57). This coaster has had an interesting history and is one of few in this book built in Norway; indeed she has strong Norwegian connections. She was built for Norwegian owners at the yard of Brødrene Lothe Flytedokken in Haugesund as *Tonja*. Sold within Norway in 1969, she was renamed *Feistein I* and another sale the following year saw her become *Samstein*. In 1976, she was sold to Swedish owners and renamed *Salome*, this being amended to *Salona* in 1977. It was in 1986 that she reverted to her original name of *Tonja*.

Die Fährstelle Breiholz liegt bei Kilometer 50, wo am 23. Juli 2002 die *Tonja* (HND, 498 BRZ/57) passiert. Das Kümo wurde unter diesem Namen im norwegischen Haugesund bei der Werft Brodrene Lothe Flytedokken gebaut. 1969 ging sie an neue Eigner, ebenfalls Norweger, die sie in *Feistein* I-70 umbenannten, bevor einem weiteren Verkauf der Name *Samstein*-76 folgte. Nun wechselte das Schiff erneut den Reeder und das erste Mal die Flagge. Als schwedische *Salome*-77 und *Salona* fuhr sie bis 1986, als ihr der Bauname wiedergegeben wurde.

(Bernard McCall)

28

Taking pilot and helmsman is compulsory on the canal for ships from a certain size and the captains of smaller vessels have to regularly renew a certificate to be granted permission to sail without. Pilots change at Rüsterbergen, between Schülp and Breiholz sidings, half-way through the canal. In this photograph we see the pilot cutter approaching the chemical tanker *Reno* (PMD, 2238gt/86), ex *Heinrich Essberger*-01, on 30 July 2004.

Auf dem Kanal besteht Lotspflicht und Schiffe ab einer bestimmten Größe müssen zusätzlich einen Kanalsteurer an Bord nehmen. Die Kapitäne kleinerer Schiffe müssen regelmäßig ihre Freifahrterlaubnis erneuern. Lotsen und Steurer wechseln in Rüsterbergen, bei Kilometer 55 zwischen den Weichen Schülp und Breiholz. Hier geht am 30. Juli 2004 gerade das Lotsenboot bei dem Chemietanker *Reno* (PMD, 2238 BRZ/86), ex *Heinrich Essberger*-01, längsseits.

(Oliver Sesemann)

Until the completion of the new facility at Rüsterbergen a few years ago, pilots changed at Schülp pilot station within the siding. It is here that this striking photo of the ro/ro vessel *Bravik* (SWE, 5173gt/74) was taken from one of the old pilot cutters. The ship belongs to the trio built at the Lindenau shipyard at Kiel described at page 23. Here she wears the colours of the forest products company Holmen Carrier whose ships can still be seen regularly on the canal. *Bravik*, however, has since been sold and changed her name to *Ivan Gorthon* as which she traded for the Swedish Gorthon shipping company until sold again in 2002 and renamed *Catumbela River*. She now sails as *Lider Safak*, flying the North Korean flag for unknown owners

Bis zum Umzug in die neue Station in Rüsterbergen fand der Lotsenwechsel in der Weiche Schülp vor der alten Lotsenstation statt, die heute als Wohngebäude dient. Von Bord eines der alten Lotsenversetzboote wurde dieses eindrucksvolle Foto des RoRo-Schiffes *Bravik* (SWE, 5173 BRZ/74) gemacht. Der Frachter ist Teil eines Trios, das von der Kieler Lindenau-Werft gebaut wurde und auf Seite 23 bereits Erwähnung fand. Hier ist er in den Farben des schwedischen Konsortiums Holmen Carrier zu sehen, dessen Schiffe noch immer regelmäßig den Kanal befahren. Die *Bravik* wurde jedoch bereits verkauft und fuhr inzwischen als *Ivan Gorthon* für die schwedische Gorthon Reederei, bis sie im Jahre 2002 weiterveräußert und in *Catumbela River* umbenannt wurde. Heute ist sie als *Lider Safak* unter nordkoreanischer Flagge unterwegs.

(Uwe Fischer)

One of the latest generation of pilot cutters has left the Rüsterbergen pilot station and approaches the **Selene Prahm** (DEU, 1584gt/94) in order to exchange pilots as she heads eastwards along the canal on 21 July 1995 when on passage from Bremen to Uusikaupunki. This coaster was built at the Kötter-Werft yard in Haren/Ems and, like all vessels in the Hammann & Prahm fleet, has been a regular sight along the canal in the last decade.

Das Lotsenboot hat soeben die neue Lotsentation in Rüsterbergen verlassen und nähert sich der **Selene Prahm** (DEU, 1584 BRZ/94), um den Brunsbütteler Lotsen gegen den Kieler Kollegen auszutauschen. Das Schiff befindet sich hier am 21. Juli 1995 auf der Reise von Bremen nach Uusikaupunki in Finnland. Wie alle Kümos der Reederei Hammann & Prahm wurde die **Selene Prahm** bei der Gebr Kötter-Werft in Haren an der Ems gebaut und ist seitdem regelmäßiger Kunde auf dem Kanal.

(Bernard McCall)

Russian ships, and this country's river/sea vessels in particular, have always been frequent callers on the canal. In this view, the *Mary-2* (RUS, 1719gt/90), ex *Nadezhda*-93, *ST-1334*-92, is seen leaving the siding at Schülp after waiting for larger oncoming ships on 1 August 2004. Two of these are the ro/ro ships *Friedrich Russ* (ATG, 10471gt/99) and *Pauline Russ* (ATG, 10488gt/99), seen in the background.

Russiche Schiffe, insbesondere die Fluss-/Seeschiffe, zählten schon immer zu den Stammkunden auf dem NOK. Am 1. August 2004 verlässt die *Mary-2* (RUS, 1719 BRZ/90), ex *Nadezhda*-93, *ST-1334*-92, westgehend die Weiche Schülp, nachdem sie auf größere Schiffe warten musste. Diese sind im Hintergrund zu sehen; es handelt sich um die RoRo-Schiffe *Friedrich Russ* (ATG, 10471 BRZ/99) and *Pauline Russ* (ATG, 10488 BRZ/99).

(Oliver Sesemann)

We stick to the subject and watch the **Ladoga-15** (RUS, 1639gt/79) on one of her countless passages, slowly approaching the siding at Schülp on 15 May 1998 - so slowly in fact that the rowing boat manages to overtake her. Both have to wait for the oncoming cruise ship **Norwegian Dream** (BHS, 50764gt/92), ex **Dreamward**-98, which is on her maiden Kiel Canal passage, accompanied by tens of thousands of onlookers.

Wir bleiben beim Thema und sehen die **Ladoga-15** (RUS, 1639 BRZ/79) am 15. Mai 1998 auf einer ihrer zahllosen Passagen langsam in die Weiche Schülp einlaufen - immerhin so langsam, dass die Ruderer an ihr vorbeiziehen. Beide müssen auf einen Gegenkommer, das Kreuzfahrtschiff **Norwegian Dream** (BHS, 50764 BRZ/92), ex **Dreamward**-98, warten. Dieses befindet sich auf seiner ersten Kanalpassage und wird von zehntausenden Sehleuten begleitet.

(Oliver Sesemann)

Rendsburg is a medium-sized town situated halfway along the canal. Here ships plough right through residential areas before passing Kreishafen harbour and the veteran railway bridge. All these places can be seen in this late afternoon view of the **Merit** (GIB, 2301gt/00) heading westwards on 6 March 2005. The ship is another example of the international structure of the business. Owned in Germany by Fahrdorfer Schiffahrts GmbH, of Schleswig, **Merit** was completed in the Netherlands by Pattje Shipyards, of Eemshaven, after her hull has been sub-contracted at the Daewoo yard in Mangalia, Romania. For operational reasons, she flies the flag of Gibraltar.

Rendsburg liegt ungefähr auf halber Strecke zwischen Brunsbüttel und Kiel. Die Schiffe pflügen hier direkt durch Wohngebiete um dann am Kreishafen vorbei unter der Eisenbahnhochbrücke hindurch zu fahren. Dies wird in dieser Perspektive auf die am 6. März 2005 westwärts gehende **Merit** (GIB, 2301 BRZ/00) deutlich. Das Schiff ist ein weiteres Beispiel für die moderne Struktur der Küstenschifffahrt: Der Eigner, Fahrdorfer Schiffahrts GmbH mit Sitz in Schleswig, ist deutsch, die Bauwerft Pattje befindet sich im niederländischen Eemshaven, der Rumpf wurde von der Daewoo Werft in Mangalia, Rumänien, zugeliefert und am Heck weht die Flagge Gibraltars.

(Oliver Sesemann)

Rendsburg has two shipyards and three quays to load and unload cargo ships. The biggest of these is Kreishafen, directly alongside the canal and near the veteran railway bridge. Here, ships of all sizes can call, mainly to load grain or receive stores. In this view it is the *Jutta-B* (DEU, 637gt/65), ex *Hendrik*-87, *Doris*-74, *Gebina*-70, which occupies a berth at the western end of the Kreishafen. The coaster was built at the Martin Jansen shipyard in Leer and was lengthened in 1974. She is a regular trader along the canal.

In Rendsburg befinden sich zwei Werften und drei Häfen für den Frachtumschlag. Der größte Umschlagsplatz ist der Kreishafen direkt am Kanal, eben westlich der alten Eisenbahnhochbrücke. Hier können Schiffe aller kanalgängigen Größen abgefertigt werden; in der Hauptsache laden sie Getreide oder übernehmen Stores. Dieses Bild zeigt die *Jutta-B* (DEU, 637 BRZ/65), ex *Hendrik*-87, *Doris*-74, *Gebina*-70 am westlichen Ende der Kaianlage. Dieser Stammkunde des Kanals wurde von der Martin Jansen-Werft im ostfriesischen Leer gebaut und 1974 verlängert.

(Bernard McCall)

It was late in the evening of 4 April 1999 when the *Gerda* (DEU, 3999gt/95) was photographed heading west and passing the *Traveberg* (GIB, 2287gt/75), ex *Patria*-94, *American Comanche*-78, berthed at Rendsburg. Both ships were built at the Neuenfelde yard of J J Sietas and represent container feeder ships of two different generations from that yard. The *Gerda* was renamed *P&O Nedlloyd Russia* for the duration of a charter between May 2002 and May 2005, when she received her former name again.

Am späten Abend des 4. April 1999 trafen sich am Rendsburger Kreishafen zwei Produkte der J. J. Sietas Werft, als der Containerfeeder *Gerda* (DEU, 3999 BRZ/95) westwärts an der *Traveberg* (GIB, 2287 BRZ/75), ex *Patria*-94, *American Comanche*-78 vorbeigleitet. Die Schiffe repräsentieren unterschiedliche Generationen von Sietas-Feedern. Im Rahmen einer späteren Charter fuhr das größere Schiff dann als *P&O Nedlloyd Russia*, wurde im Jahre 2005 jedoch wieder in *Gerda* umbenannt.

(Bernard McCall)

The railway bridge at Rendsburg is situated at the eastern end of the Kreishafen. Built during the first extension of the canal between 1911 and 1913, it features a "ferry" which is fixed with cables to special rails on the bridge and hovers across the canal directly underneath, without ever touching water. The usual English term is "transporter bridge". One of eight such bridges in the world, it is preserved as a technical monument. On 5 August 2004 we see the *Monika* (ATG, 1768gt/77), ex *Mona Rosa*-04, *Stepenitz*-99, *Noordland*-89, passing the bridge with one of the Kreishafen silos in the background. She is another Dutch-built coaster, constructed by the Scheepswerf G. Bijlsma & Zn. BV in Wartena and is owned in Drochtersen by Günter Bahr.

Die Rendsburger Eisenbahnhochbrücke befindet sich am östlichen Ende des Kreishafens. Sie entstand im Rahmen der ersten Kanalerweiterung zwischen 1911 und 1913 und ist berühmt nicht nur für ihre Stahlkonstruktion sondern insbesondere auch wegen der Schwebefähre, die an Kabeln unter der Brücke hängt und niemals das Wasser berührt. Das technische Denkmal ist eines von nur noch acht Exemplaren auf der Welt. Am 5. August 2004 passiert die *Monika* (ATG, 1768 BRZ/77), ex *Mona Rosa*-04, *Stepenitz*-99, *Noordland*-89, das Bauwerk. Im Hintergrund ist eines der Silos am Kreishafen zu sehen. *Monika* ist ein weiteres in den Niederlanden entstandenes Schiff, das bei der Scheepswerf G. Bijlsma & Zn. BV in Wartena gebaut wurde. Es gehört dem Reeder Günter Bahr aus Drochtersen.

(Oliver Sesemann)

Another of the three quays in Rendsburg makes use of a part of the Eider river. At the Audorf/Rade siding, a two kilometre stretch of river branches off and forms the Obereiderhafen area. At its remote end we see the veteran **Mobby Dick** (HND, 203gt/52), ex **Lindholm**-03, **Ingrid**-52, awaiting orders on 17 February 2005. Like a number of other ships in this book, she is a product of the Hugo Peters shipyard at Wewelsfleth. It is her recent history, however, which has attracted considerable interest. After a delivery voyage from Denmark to the Caribbean ended at a buoy in the Elbe estuary far from the intended route, the **Lindholm** was taken to Cuxhaven and then laid up in Wischhafen from where she was eventually brought back into service under her new name. Clearly **Mobby Dick** has succeeded thus far in withstanding all attempts to make her leave her north European home waters!

Ein weiterer der drei Kais in Rendsburg, der Obereiderhafen, liegt an einer zwei Kilometer langen Abzweigung der Eider, deren Verlauf der Kanal teilweise folgt. Hier liegt am 17. Februar 2005 der Veteran **Mobby Dick** (HND, 203 BRZ/52), ex **Lindholm**-03, **Ingrid**-52, und wartet auf die nächste Order. Wie einige der Schiffe auf diesen Seiten auch, wurde dieses Kümo einst bei der Werft Hugo Peters in Wewelsfleth erbaut. Es ist aber insbesondere seine jüngste Vergangenheit, die für Aufmerksamkeit sorgte. Nach dem Verkauf in Dänemark im Sommer 2003 endete die Ablieferungsfahrt mit Ziel Karibik weit entfernt davon an einer Fahrwassertonne der Elbmündung. Es folgte eine Aufliegezeit in Wischhafen, wo die **Lindholm** auf der Ewer Werft geflickt, blau angepönt und in **Mobby Dick** umbenannt wurde. Wieder in Nord- und Ostsee im Einsatz war ihr Widerstand gegen eine Verlegung weitab der Heimatgewässer eindeutig von Erfolg gekrönt!

(Oliver Sesemann)

Just east of Rendsburg the canal makes use of a former lake and the river Eider, resulting in the large twin siding of Audorf and Rade. It is at the western end of this siding that we see the *Nona* (NLD, 1978gt/02), approaching the Nobiskrug ferry landing on 6 August 2004. The photograph was taken from a dedicated, elevated viewing area in Schacht-Audorf. Built by the Niestern Sander shipyard, *Nona* is another example of successful and innovative Dutch coaster design. She belongs to the extensive fleet of Wijnne & Barends Cargadoors- en agentuurskantoren BV, of Delfzijl, whose ships are a daily sight on the canal.

Eben östlich von Rendsburg verläuft das Kanalbett durch den Audorfer und den Schirnauer See sowie das alte Bett der Eider. Hier befindet sich die sog. „Großweiche" Audorf/Rade, an deren westlichem Ende am 5. August 2004 die *Nona* (NLD, 1978 BRZ/02) auf die Fährstelle Nobiskrug zuläuft. An dieser Stelle ermöglicht ein erhöhter Aussichtspunkt einen guten Überblick über das Geschehen auf dem Kanal. *Nona*, gebaut bei der Niestern Sander-Werft, repräsentiert den erfolgreichen, innovativen Schiffbau der Niederlande. Sie gehört zu der großen Flotte der Reederei Wijnne & Barends Cargadoors- en agentuurskantoren BV in Delfzijl, deren leuchtend orangefarbene Schiffe täglich den NOK nutzen.

(Oliver Sesemann)

Seen from the opposite bank is the former Krögerwerft shipyard in Schacht-Audorf. A subsidiary of the Lürssen Werft in Bremen, the yard today specialises in the construction of large yachts. In Krögerwerft days, however, the facilities were the birthplace of many cargo ships, some of which are featured in this book (q.v.). Seen fitting out at the yard on 5 August 1998 is the container feeder *Heike* (GBR, 2988gt/98). She is one of four of her type built for the Rendsburg-based Reederei Karl Schlüter, who have their offices just a few kilometres down the canal. The German cruise ship *Europa* (BHS, 37301gt/81) is sneaking around the corner, waiting for oncoming traffic. This vessel now trades mainly in Europe as *Holiday Dream* after pioneering spells in east Asia as *Superstar Aries* and *Superstar Europe*.

Vom gegenüberliegenden Kanalufer ist an dieser Stelle die ehemalige Krögerwerft in Schacht-Audorf zu sehen. Hier werden heute Superyachten konstruiert, da die Anlagen von der Bremer Lürssen Werft übernommen wurden. Als hier noch die Krögerwerft Schiffe baute, entstanden zahlreiche Frachtschiffe, die z.T. heute noch den Kanal befahren. Am 5. August 1998 liegt hier der Containerfeeder *Heike* (GBR, 2988 BRZ/98) an der Ausrüstungspier. Das Schiff ist eines von vier Schwesterschiffen, die für die Rendsburger Reederei Karl Schlüter gebaut wurden. Im Hintergrund schleicht das Kreuzfahrtschiff *Europa* (BHS, 37301 BRZ/81) um die Ecke, das auf Gegenkommer warten muss. Nach einigen Jahren als Pionier auf dem ostasiatischen Markt, wo es unter den Namen *Superstar Europe*-00 und *Superstar Aries*-04 fuhr, ist das Schiff nunmehr als *Holiday Dream* in Europa stationiert.

(Oliver Sesemann)

On 27 May 1997, the Sietas-built *Passaden* (FIN, 3828gt/91) heads eastwards along the canal past Schacht-Audorf, with the Kröger Werft yard in the background to the left of the photograph. She was on passage to Turku and Mantyluoto from Hamburg and Bremerhaven, her usual route. Completed as *Passaden*, this ship was renamed *ECL Captain* shortly after entry into service but reverted to her original name in 1992.

Am 27. Mai 1997 fährt die *Passaden* (FIN, 3828 BRZ/91), ein weiteres Produkt der J.J. Sietas-Werft, an den Anlagen der Kröger-Werft in Schacht-Audorf vorbei in östliche Richtung. Sie war unterwegs auf einer ihrer vielen Rundreisen von Hamburg und Bremerhaven nach Mantyluoto in Finnland. Kurz nach Indienststellung fuhr das Schiff ein Jahr lang als *ECL Captain*-92, trägt seitdem jedoch wieder seinen Baunamen.

(Bernard McCall)

Shortly after passing the attractive canalside village of Sehestedt where another vehicle ferry crosses the waterway, the low air-draught coaster *Alissa* (NLD, 1170gt/96) is approaching the large Audorf/Rade siding on the cold afternoon of 29 December 2004. Owned by Hamburg-based Ewald Müller & Co. GmbH, the coaster is operated by the Dutch Wagenborg Shipping company and was built by the Schloemer shipyard of Oldersum.

Zwischen dem kleinen Ort Sehestedt, wo sich eine weitere Fährstelle befindet, und der Großweiche Rade/Audorf gleitet am Nachmittag des kalten 29. Dezember 2004 die *Alissa* (NLD, 1170 BRZ/96) durch das stille Wasser. Das Schiff gehört der Hamburger Reederei Ewald Müller & Co. GmbH und ist an die niederländische Wagenborg Reederei verchartert. Gebaut wurde *Alissa* auf der Schloemer-Werft in Oldersum.

(Oliver Sesemann)

Between Brunsbüttel and Königsförde, the canal runs fairly straight; this has made extension works relatively easy. On the last 20 km, east of the Königsförde siding, however, the canal is winding its way among the hills which has prevented similar measures so far. Only the recent rise in ship passages and brisk market outlooks for the Baltic have sparked renewed interest in the extension of this final part. Seen leaving this section on 22 June 1998 is the *Carolina* (NIS, 1583gt/72), ex *Bellatrix*-89, *Thies*-84, and since renamed *Lisbeth*, built at the J J Sietas shipyard. This ship features a gantry crane typical of Scandinavia's aggregates trades.

Da der Kanal zwischen Brunsbüttel und Königsförde einen recht geraden Verlauf hat und größtenteils flaches Land und relativ lockeren Geestboden durchquert, konnte er auf diesem Stück ab 1965 bereits ausgebaut werden. Die letzten 20 Kilometer zwischen Königsförde und Kiel jedoch verlaufen kurvenreich durch den härteren Boden des östlichen Hügellandes, was einen Ausbau bisher verhinderte. Der Anstieg der Passagezahlen und entsprechende Prognosen sind nun der Auslöser für verstärkte Forderungen nach einer Erweiterung auch dieses Teilstücks, das die *Carolina* (NIS, 1583 BRZ/72), ex *Bellatrix*-89, *Thies*-84, inzwischen *Lisbeth*, am 22. Juni 1998 in Richtung Westen verlässt. Das bei J. J. Sietas gebaute Schiff wurde mit einem Baggerkran für Lockermaterialientransporte nachgerüstet.

(Oliver Sesemann)

The small ships built to renew the German coaster fleet after WW2 are often termed the "nuclei" of a rapid development of successful coastal ship designs out of which eventually grew one of today's most modern fleets. One such "germ-cell" certainly is the *Iris-Jörg* (DEU, 281gt/56), ex *Seestern*-65, *Eilenburg*-64, built by the canalside shipyard Werft Nobiskrug GmbH in Rendsburg. Seen here on 23 June 1996, passing the siding at Königsförde on an eastbound voyage during one of her last years in active cargo shipping, the vessel is now used as a museum ship based in Wischhafen on the river Elbe.

Die Kümos, die nach dem Zweiten Weltkrieg unter den einschränkenden Regeln der Siegermächte entstanden, werden heute häufig als die Keimzelle des modernen deutschen Schiffbaus und der Handelsflotte bezeichnet. Zu ihnen gehört in jedem Falle die *Iris-Jörg* (DEU, 281 BRZ/56), ex *Seestern*-65, *Eilenburg*-64, die sogar am Kanal bei der Werft Nobiskrug GmbH in Rendsburg entstanden ist. Das Schiff passiert hier am 23 Juni 1996 ostwärts die Weiche Königsförde während ihrer letzten Dienstjahre als aktives Frachtschiff. *Iris-Jörg* dient heute als Museumsschiff in Wischhafen im Alten Land.

(Oliver Sesemann)

It is not often that winters are so strong that ice develops on the canal. However, a particularly cold winter was that of 1978/79 when easterly winds pushed the ice from the north-eastern Baltic down to its western shores. All of the Kieler Förde fjord was frozen and a large part of the Kiel Canal was affected by ice floes. Here we see the container feeder *Diana* (DEU, 3004gt/75) making her way past a large freighter at the Königsförde siding. This ship's later career can be followed earlier in the book (p. 16) where she is featured under one of her later names.

Es kommt nicht häufig vor, dass sich auf dem Kanal Eis bildet. Einer dieser strengen Winter war 1978/79, als östliche Winde das Eis der nordöstlichen Ostsee bis an den westlichen Rand drückten und so die Kieler Förde vollständig zufror. Auch auf dem Kanal bildete sich Eis. Hier bahnt sich der Containerfeeder *Diana* (DEU, 3004 BRZ/75) seinen Weg durch die Schollen, vorbei an einem größeren Frachter in der Weiche Königsförde. Eine Beschreibung der weiteren Karriere des Schiffes kann auf Seite 16 nachgelesen werden, wo das Schiff als *Hege* erscheint.

(Uwe Fischer)

Despite compulsory pilotage and regular renewals of certificates for small ships to sail without, the narrow confines of the canal sometimes cause collisions or ships touching the canal's banks. It was the underwater remains of an old jetty in the Groß-Nordsee siding which cut open the hull of the coaster **Detlef Schmidt** (DEU, 499gt/63) as seen in this undated view. Most collisions, however, turn out not to be too serious. This coaster was built at the Büsumer Schiffswerft shipyard in Büsum and traded as **Coast Ranger** before being scrapped in the UK in 1994.

Obwohl Lotspflicht besteht und Kapitäne kleinerer Schiffe regelmäßig ihre Freifahrterlaubnis erneuern müssen, kommt es in den engen Gewässern des Kanals gelegentlich zu Kollisionen oder Böschungsberührungen. In diesem Falle waren es die unter Wasser liegenden Reste eines alten Anlegers in der Weiche Groß-Nordsee, die den Rumpf der **Detlef Schmidt** (DEU, 499 BRZ/63) aufschlitzten. Die meisten Kollisionen laufen jedoch glimpflich ab. Das hier illustrierte Schiff wurde auf der Büsumer Werft gebaut und fuhr später als **Coast Ranger**, bevor es 1994 in Großbritannien verschrottet wurde.

(Uwe Fischer)

The ferry crossing at Landwehr is located 87 km along the canal from Brunsbüttel. The diminutive **Tina** (DEU, 328gt/60), ex **Timo**-94, **Freiheit**-78, heads westwards from the Danish port of Nykøbing on 30 March 1999. Built by J J Sietas, this small vessel was lengthened in 1969, and then lengthened and deepened in 1982.

Die Fährstelle Landwehr liegt eben östlich der Weiche Groß-Nordsee, bei Kanalkilometer 87. Unterwegs vom dänischen Nykøbing am 30. März 1999 ist hier die kleine **Tina** (DEU, 328 BRZ/60), ex **Timo**-94, **Freiheit**-78, zu sehen. Dieses ebenfalls bei J. J. Sietas entstandene Schiff wurde, wie viele Kümos im Laufe ihrer Karriere, zweimal verlängert, nämlich 1969 und 1982, als auch der Tiefgang vergrößert wurde.

(Bernard McCall)

Ships built by the J J Sietas shipyard near Hamburg are a common sight on the canal, particularly many of the modern container feeders. But the yard was successful long before the age of the box. Representative of its classic 1960s style of coaster of which there is still a number of exemplars around is the **Mignon** (ATG, 1069gt/66), ex **Jana**-97, **Jan Suhr**-81, **Siegerland**-74. As part of the Type 33 series, she had originally been equipped with her own cargo-handling gear. She is seen heading westwards on 30 March 1999.

Viele Schiffe, die regelmäßig den NOK passieren, wurden von der Werft J. J. Sietas erbaut. Darunter befinden sich nicht nur moderne Containerschiffe sondern auch noch zahlreiche klassische Kümos aus einer Zeit vor dem Siegeszug des Containers. Beispielhaft für das Sietas-Kümo der 1960er Jahre soll die **Mignon** (ATG, 1069 BRZ/66), ex **Jana**-97, **Jan Suhr**-81, **Siegerland**-74, des Werfttyps 33 stehen. Ursprünglich waren diese Schiffe auch mit eigenem Ladegeschirr ausgerüstet.

(Bernard McCall)

This picture of the **Beta** (DEU, 1064gt/67), ex **Betty**-97, **Rolf**-85, seen here approaching the Levensau bridges in ballast on 7 April 2002, clearly emphasises the term "classic" used for the **Mignon**. And indeed, the **Beta** is number 19 of 29 built of Sietas Type 33.

Die Bezeichnung „klassisch" auf der vorherigen Seite wird eindeutig durch dieses Bild der **Beta** (DEU, 1064 BRZ/67), ex **Betty**-97, **Rolf**-85, unterstrichen. Die Nummer 19 von 29 gebauten Einheiten des Typs 33 nähert sich hier am 7. April 2002 auf einer Ballastfahrt rauschend den Levensauer Brücken.

(Oliver Sesemann)

Approaching the Levensau bridges on 29 May 2005 is the *Weser Highway* (PAN, 8659gt/93). She is on one of her regular passages along the canal, delivering Volkswagen vehicles from Bremerhaven to Halmstad. She calls at Emden and Grimsby before returning to Bremerhaven. Built by K K Usuki Zosensho at Usuki in Japan and able to carry 805 cars, she traded as *Feedercaptain* for E H Harms Reederei until taking her current name in late August 2004. E H Harms is a freight forwarder for the automobile industry and has employed ships to distribute cars throughout northern Europe. When the company withdrew from shipowning in 2004, its vessels were taken over by former joint-venture partner K-Line who now continue to operate the route network as part of their K-Line European Short Sea Services (K.E.S.S.). Although she is not a conventional coaster in appearance, *Weser Highway*'s trading pattern and length of just under 100 metres certainly allow her to be called a coaster.

Mit einer Ladung Volkswagen erreicht die *Weser Highway* (PAN, 8659 BRZ/93), ex *Feedercaptain*-04, am 29. Mai 2005 auf dem Weg von Bremerhaven nach Halmstad die Levensauer Hochbrücken. Ihre regelmäßigen Rundreisen führen sie noch nach Grimsby und Emden, bevor sie wieder in Bremerhaven eintrifft. Der bei K. K. Usuki Zosensho im japanischen Usuki gebaute und für 805 PKW ausgelegte Autotransporter fuhr seit seiner Indienststellung in Charter der deutschen Automobilspedition E. H. Harms als *Feedercaptain.* Nachdem Harms jedoch im Jahre 2004 das Schifffahrtsgeschäft einstellte, um sich nur noch auf seine LKW-Flotte zu konzentrieren, wurden die Schiffe vollständig durch den bisherigen Joint-Venture-Partner, die japanische K-Line, übernommen. Die Liniendienste werden jetzt unter dem Namen KESS (K-Line European Short Sea Services) mit erweiterter Flotte fortgeführt. Obwohl das Profil der *Weser Highway* nicht dem eines konventionellen Kümos entspricht, erlauben ihr Einsatz in nordeuropäischen Shortsea-Verkehren sowie ihre begrenzten Maße dennoch die Einordnung als Küstenmotorschiff im weiteren Sinne.

(Bernard McCall)

The eastern end of the canal offers some very popular vantage points for ship photography. One of these is the area near the Levensau bridge which carries the B76 road from Kiel to Eckernförde. Alongside the road bridge is one of the first fixed crossings of the canal, the old bridge carrying the railway line which serves these two conurbations as well as a minor road. It is the latter bridge which towers above the *Lizrix* (BHS, 2019gt/77), ex *Yorksee*-96, *Katharina*-90, *Karlsvik*-86, as she heads to Riga from Hull on 11 September 2000.

Die Oststrecke mit ihrer hügeligen Landschaft bietet eine Vielzahl schöner Aussichtspunkte, um den Kanalverkehr zu beobachten. Eine sehr populäre Stelle liegt an den Levensauer Hochbrücken. Während die neue Brücke die B 76 über den Kanal führt und nicht begehbar ist, ermöglicht die Zugänglichkeit der alten Levensauer Brücke dem Betrachter zahlreiche Perspektiven. Diese Brücke, die baugleich mit der 1986 ersetzten Grünentaler Brücke ist und eine der ersten festen Querungen über dem Kanal war, thront hier am 11. September 2000 über der *Lizrix* (BHS, 2019 BRZ/77), ex *Yorksee*-96, *Katharina*-90, *Karlsvik*-86. Das Schiff war unterwegs vom nordenglischen Hull, Sitz der Reederei Rix Shipping, nach Riga.

(Oliver Sesemann)

With both Levensau bridges in view, we see the **Karin Lehmann** (ATG, 2820gt/00) heading westwards and approaching the Schwartenbek siding on 21 April 2002. With her distinctive bright green hull paint the ship belongs to the Lübeck-based Reederei Lehmann KG and is employed in European coastal shipping. She was built by the Frisian Shipyard Welgelegen of Harlingen.

Am 21. April 2002 passiert die **Karin Lehmann** (ATG, 2820 BRZ/00) die Levensauer Hochbrücken in Richtung Weiche Schwartenbek. Die leuchtend grüne Farbe ihres Rumpfes ist das Markenzeichen der Lübecker Reederei Lehmann KG, deren Schiffe überwiegend in der europäischen Küstenschifffahrt eingesetzt werden. **Karin Lehmann** ist ein Produkt der Frisian Shipyard Welgelegen im niederländischen Harlingen.

(Oliver Sesemann)

With both bridges in view, we see the **Lupus** (DIS, 2709gt/74), ex **Kronholm**-00, **Weser**-99, heading eastwards to Hamburg and Bremerhaven from Gdynia and Gdansk. Built by J J Sietas and of this company's Type 83, she is owned by Stüwe & Co, a Hamburg-based shipbroking company, and operated by CJ Shipping, of Denmark. At the time of the photograph, her voyages to Poland alternated with voyages to Esbjerg. The date is 21 April 2002.

Ein weiterer Blick von halber Höhe auf den Kanal und beide Levensauer Brücken zeigt hier am 21. April 2002 den ostwärts fahrenden Containerzubringer **Lupus** (DIS, 2709 BRZ/74), ex **Kronholm**-00, **Weser**-99, auf seiner regelmäßigen Rundreise zwischen Hamburg, Bremerhaven und Gdynia in Polen. Zum Zeitpunkt der Aufnahme alternierten die Routen, teilweise wurde auch Esbjerg angelaufen. Dieser frühe Feedertyp der J. J. Sietas-Werft (Typ 83) gehört zur Flotte des Hamburger Shipbrokers Stüwe & Co., der das Schiff an die dänische CJ Shipping verchartert hat.

(Oliver Sesemann)

In the 1990s, the Kröger-Werft shipyard of Schacht-Audorf, near Rendsburg, had introduced a successful container feeder design of which they completed fourteen vessels. Four of these were built for Chinese owners before the design was sold to China as well. Ten ships were delivered to various German owners who chartered them to northern European feeder operators. Two of these vessels, **Ute Johanna** (DEU, 2984gt/95) and **Ute** (DEU, 2988gt/99), since renamed **Ute S**, are seen here passing the Levensau bridges on their weekly routes from the Baltic in June 1999.

In den 1990er Jahren hat die Kröger Werft in Schacht-Audorf eine erfolgreiche Serie von 14 Containerfeedern gebaut. Vier von diesen gingen an chinesische Eigner, bevor auch die Pläne nach Fernost verkauft wurden. Zehn Einheiten baute die Werft für eine Reihe deutscher Reedereien, die die Schiffe meist an nordeuropäische Feeder-Gesellschaften verchartern konnten. Zwei Schwesterschiffe aus dieser Serie, die **Ute Johanna** (DEU, 2984 BRZ/95) und **Ute** (DEU, 2988 BRZ/99), inzwischen **Ute S**, passieren hier im Juni 1999 die Levensauer Brücken auf ihren wöchentlichen Rundreisen.

(Oliver Sesemann)

Passing the bend between Schwartenbek and Nordhafen sidings on 21 April 2002 is the Estonian-owned **Sylve** (CYP, 1999gt/90), ex **Vios**-01, **Morgenstond II**-97, a ship of obvious Dutch origins; and indeed, she was built by Ferus Smit BV at Westerbroek. Following her is the **Pavo** (ATG, 3300gt/86), ex **Normed Istanbul**-01, **Pavo**-00, **Seevetal**-98, another product of the J J Sietas shipyard.

Die estnische **Sylve** (CYP, 1999 BRZ/90), ex **Vios**-01, **Morgenstond II**-97, hat die typischen Linien eines modernen niederländischen Kümos. Sie wurde von Ferus Smit BV gebaut und fuhr lange Zeit für die Reederei Wijnne & Barends Cargadoors- en agentuurskantoren BV in Delfzijl. Durch die Kurve zwischen Schwartenbek und dem Nordhafen folgt ihr am 21. April 2002 die bei J. J. Sietas entstandene **Pavo** (ATG, 3300 BRZ/86), ex **Normed Istanbul**-01, **Pavo**-00, **Seevetal**-98.

(Oliver Sesemann)

Along with the disappearance of the Eastern bloc, Soviet vessels have become less frequent callers on the canal. The Russian successor companies soon sold off much of the old tonnage so it was one of the last occasions when the veteran Russian tanker **Beta** (RUS, 2978gt/61), ex **Elgava**, seen here between Nordhafen and Schwartenbek sidings, passed through on a westbound voyage on 27 June 1996. The veteran eventually left the Baltic, sailing from Liepaja bound for India on 19 May 1998. In the 1950s and 1960s, the Finnish Rauma-Repola O/Y yard had built two similar series of tankers of which a total of at least 42 were delivered. Built by Gävle Varv shipyard of Gefle, Sweden, two tankers of a nearly identical design were added. It is the latter version the **Beta** belongs to.

Mit dem Zusammenbruch des Ostblocks kamen nach und nach auch immer weniger Schiffe seiner Handelsflotten, die dereinst zu den treuesten Kunden des Kanals zählten. Schnell veräußerten die Nachfolgegesellschaften veraltete Tonnage und so war es eine der letzten Gelegenheiten, den russischen Veteranen **Beta** (RUS, 2978 BRZ/61), ex **Elgava**, im aktiven Dienst zu sehen, als der Tanker am 27. Juni 1996 westgehend die Kurve zwischen Levensauer Brücken und dem Nordhafen passierte. Endgültig verließ dieses Schiff die Ostsee dann im Jahre 1998, als es am 19. Mai von Liepaja gen Indien versegelte. In den 1950er und '60er Jahren baute die finnische Werft Rauma Repola O/Y zwei sehr ähnliche Serien von insgesamt mindestens 42 Einheiten. Zwei weitere verwandte Tanker kamen von der schwedischen Gävle Varv, darunter die **Beta** unter ihrem Baunamen **Elgava**.

(Oliver Sesemann)

There are several bunkering jetties at the eastern end of the canal. The **Merle** (DEU, 510gt/80), built by C Lühring at Brake, is often seen on the canal and she loads bunker fuel to deliver to vessels in other German ports. She was photographed at the Total bunker berth on 14 July 1999.

Am östlichen Ende des Kanals in Kiel befindet sich auf der Südseite eine Reihe von Hafenanlagen. Westlich der Weiche Nordhafen, in der bewaldeten Kurve nach Schwartenbek, liegt die Total-Bunkerstation. Hier legt am 14. Juli 1999 das kleine Bunkerschiff **Merle** (DEU, 510 BRZ/80), das zu den treuesten Kunden des NOK gehört. **Merle** wurde bei der Werft C. Lühring in Brake an der Weser erbaut.

(Bernard McCall)

Yet another feeder ship to be seen frequently on the canal is the *Holstein* (DEU, 3815gt/91). Built by J J Sietas as *Holstein*, some of her previous names provide a good indication of her charterers for she became *Schleswig-Holstein* on entry into service in 1991, then *ECL Commander* briefly in also 1991, *Nordic Bridge* still in 1991, *Gracechurch Planet* in 1994, and then *Holstein* once again in 1996. The passing yacht and the family on the canal bank provide a good illustration of the importance of the canal for leisure purposes. The photograph was taken on 4 April 1999.

Ein weiteres Feederschiff, ein weiterer Stammkunde: Die *Holstein* (DEU, 3815 BRZ/91) repräsentiert einen typischen Lebenslauf in der heutigen Containerzubringerfahrt. Sie wurde 1991 von J. J. Sietas als *Schleswig-Holstein* abgeliefert, wechselte aufgrund einer Charter schnell den Namen in *ECL Commander* und fuhr noch im selben Jahr als *Nordic Bridge* unter einem Namen, den sie bis 1994 führte. Ein weiterer Chartername war *Gracechurch Planet*, bevor das Schiff 1996 wieder seinen - verkürzten - Baunamen *Holstein* und als Heimathafen Rendsburg bekam. Die Bedeutung des Nord-Ostsee-Kanals für den Freizeit- und Tourismussektor, die weiter oben bereits betont wurde, wird auch in diesem Foto vom 4. April 1999 besonders deutlich.

(Bernard McCall)

A busy scene on 5 August 2003 as the **Ek-Sky** (NIS, 8828gt/99), built at the Jiangnan Shipyard in Shanghai, heads westwards from Brofjorden and passes two coasters heading east towards the locks at Holtenau. Just visible is the bow of the **Drawa** (POL, 1575gt/78) which was heading to the Danish port of Fakse Ladeplads having discharged a cargo of limestone from there at Rendsburg earlier in the day. Also visible is the **Paaschburg** (ATG, 3228gt/80) heading for Gothenburg from Hamburg and Bremerhaven.

Eine geschäftige Szene sich begegnender Einheiten im Nordhafen Kiel am 5. August 2003 verdeutlicht die Funktion der Weichen als Begegnungsstellen. Der Tanker **Ek-Sky** (NIS, 8828 BRZ/99), ein Produkt der aufstrebenden Jiangnan Werft in Schanghai, passiert von Brofjorden kommend westwärts den Kanal und an dieser Stelle zwei entgegenkommende Kümos. Gerade ins Bild fährt die **Drawa** (POL, 1575 BRZ/78), die bis kurz zuvor eine Ladung Kalkstein im Rendsburger Kreishafen gelöscht hatte und nun auf dem Rückweg ins dänische Fakse Ladeplads ist. Der Feeder **Paaschburg** (ATG, 3328 BRZ/80) befindet sich auf dem Weg von Hamburg und Bremerhaven nach Göteborg.

(Bernard McCall)

A photograph of historical interest taken on 13 August 1995. The high-level bridge (Straßenhochbrücke) carries the B503 road from Kiel to Eckernförde and one of its spans was was put in place at the time of the photograph which shows the work underway. The *Dürnstein* (AUT, 2367gt/86), built as *Visurgis* by Herman Sürken at Papenburg, had been renamed only two weeks previously.

Ein geschichtliches Dokument stellt dieses Bild vom 13. August 1995 dar. Nachdem die alte Holtenauer Hochbrücke aus Altersgründen abgebaut werden musste, entstand an gleicher Stelle ein Ersatz neben der - nun „alten" - Olympiabrücke. Während der Konstruktionsphase passiert hier die österreichische *Dürnstein* (AUT, 2367 BRZ/86) die Baustelle in luftiger Höhe. Gebaut auf der Werft Hermann Sürken in Papenburg als *Visurgis*, wurde das Schiff nur zwei Wochen vor der Aufnahme umbenannt.

(Bernard McCall)

David and Goliath often meet on the canal. On this occasion the small tanker *Finja* (DEU, 942gt/00) is heading west through the Nordhafen siding at Kiel on 24 March 2002 passing the eastbound tanker *Luctor* (SGP, 22607gt/91), ex *Luctor 2*-96, *Team Heina*-95, *Faith*-91, launched as *Mosor Sun*. The former belongs to the fleet of Cuxhaven-based Reimer Glüsing whose ships can frequently be seen on the canal loading bunker fuel at Kiel or Brunsbüttel for delivery to vessels in other German ports. *Finja* was built in Rumania by Santierul Naval SA.

David und Goliath treffen im Kanal täglich aufeinander. In diesem Falle sind es der kleine Tanker *Finja* (DEU, 942 BRZ/00), auf einer Reise von Kiel nach Brunsbüttel, und der große Tanker *Luctor* (SGP, 22607 BRZ/91), ex *Luctor 2*-96, *Team Heina*-95, *Faith*-91, vom Stapel als *Mosor Sun*, die sich am 24. März 2002 im Nordhafen begegnen. *Finja* gehört zur Flotte des Cuxhavener Reeders Reimer Glüsing, dessen Schiffe überwiegend als Bunkerbargen in deutschen Häfen arbeiten und zu den Stammkunden auf dem NOK zählen. Glüsing ließ diesen Tanker bei der rumänischen Werft Santierul Naval SA bauen.

(Oliver Sesemann)

The same vantage point but looking south provides this busy view of a part of Nordhafen. Heading westwards on a rather overcast 3 November 2000 is the **Edda** (CYP, 2729gt/85), ex **Torm Tema**-98, **Edda**-97, built by the Martin Jansen shipyard in Leer and featuring two 25-tonne cranes. She now sails as **Kotkas**. In the background an array of Kiel Canal regulars is berthed. The tanker **Margaron** (SWE, 1003gt/70), ex **Regine**-84, is loading rape oil and taking bunkers from the local barge **O.W. Bunker I** while the **Mistral** (ATG, 1064gt/66), ex **Nadine**-98, **Ragna**-90, **Tilla**-83, **Süderelv**-78, **Frieda Graebe**-73, is discharging her load of grain. The small **Steen** (ATG, 328gt/61), ex **Ingrid I**-82, **Steenborg**-81, has to await her turn. All three vessels have been built in Germany, the tanker at Bayerische Schiffbau GmbH on the river Main, the other pair by J J Sietas and Hugo Peters, respectively.

Derselbe Standort und eine andere Blickrichtung bieten diese Aussicht auf das Nordhafensilo. An einem trüben 3. November 2000 passiert die bei der Martin Jansen Werft in Leer gebaute und mit zwei 25-Tonnen-Kranen ausgerüstete **Edda** (CYP, 2729 BRZ/85), heute **Kotkas**, ex **Torm Tema**-98, **Edda**-97, westwärts drei Kanalstammkunden. Der Tanker **Margaron** (SWE, 1003 BRZ/70), ex **Regine**-84, lädt gerade Rapsöl und übernimmt Bunker von der Barge **O.W. Bunker I**, während die **Mistral** (ATG, 1064 BRZ/66), ex **Nadine**-98, **Ragna**-90, **Tilla**-83, **Süderelv**-78, **Frieda Graebe**-73, ihre Getreideladung löscht und die kleine **Steen** (ATG, 328 BRZ/61), ex **Ingrid I**-82, **Steenborg**-81, auf deren Liegeplatz wartet. Diese drei Kümos wurden dereinst alle auf deutschen Werften gebaut. Der Tanker entstand bei der Bayerische Schiffbau GmbH in Erlenbach/Main, die beiden anderen Kümos bei J. J. Sietas, Neuenfelde, bzw. Hugo Peters, Wewelsfleth.

(Oliver Sesemann)

Seen from below the bridges, the immaculately-kept *Arngast* (DEU, 833gt/58), ex *Beta*-97, *Drochtersen*-91, *Baltica*-75, *Weser*-64, is heading westwards past the Nordhafen silo on 29 February 2002. The bulker *Adamandas* (CYP, 14487gt/86) is loading grain which had been brought beforehand by the likes of *Arngast*. This small ship is typical of the many veteran coasters which despite their age are still busy in the agriculture trades of the western Baltic and German Bight ports. She was built by C. Lühring Schiffswerft in Brake on the river Weser.

Das Friedrich-Voss-Ufer in Holtenau bietet unter den Brücken diese Aussicht. Am 29. Februar 2002 ist die westgehende *Arngast* (DEU, 833 BRZ/58), ex *Beta*-97, *Drochtersen*-91, *Baltica*-75, *Weser*-64, der Blickfang als sie am frühen Morgen den Bulker *Adamandas* (CYP, 14487 BRZ/86) passiert, der am Nordhafen-Silo Getreide lädt. Dieses landwirtschaftliche Produkt wird in der Regel von Kümos wie eben der *Arngast* aus der Region für den Export herangebracht. Die stets gut in Schuss gehaltene *Arngast* ist typisch für die zahlreichen älteren kleinen coaster, die in diesem Handel eingesetzt sind. Sie wurde auf der C. Lühring Schiffswerft in Brake/Weser gebaut.

(Oliver Sesemann)

The Holtenau high level bridge is hugely popular with ship enthusiasts and casual onlookers. Looking eastwards from the bridge on the evening of 1 August 1991, we find a very busy scene. The *Köthen* (DEU, 6171gt/78), built at Rostock for the former East German state-owned shipping company, had been delayed in leaving the lock for her westbound passage and a traffic jam soon built up. In the far distance is the Kieler Förde. At that time the locks to the left, the Alte Schleusen (Old Locks), were used almost exclusively by pleasure craft while those to the right, the Neue Schleusen (New Locks), were reserved for commercial vessels. The *Baltiyskiy 60* (RUS, 1872gt/66) is the last of five ships heading for the northern lock of the Neue Schleusen. She is returning to the Baltic from Shoreham.

Die Holtenauer Hochbrücken sind bekannte Aussichtspunkte in Kiel. Von der östlichen Brücke bietet sich dieser Blick - nach Osten - auf den Binnenhafen und die Schleusenanlagen - links die alten, rechts die neuen Kammern - mit der Förde im Hintergrund. Die nostalgische Aufnahme vom 1. August 1991 zeigt den ehemaligen DDR-Frachter *Köthen* (DEU, 6171 BRZ/78), gebaut für die Deutsche Seereederei in Rostock. Nach dem Auslaufen macht er hier die neue Nordkammer frei für eine Gruppe von fünf ostgehenden Schiffen, darunter das russische Fluss-/Seeschiff *Baltiyskiy 60* (RUS, 1872 BRZ/66) auf dem Weg von Shoreham in die Ostsee. Ein Jahr nachdem die DDR in der Bundesrepublik aufging, zerfiel auch die Sowjetunion, so muss dies eine der ersten Aufnahmen des Schiffes unter russischer Flagge sein.

(Bernard McCall)

Seen from the same vantage point, it is another typical scene when the **Debora** (NIS, 2331gt/65), ex **Porrino**-90, **Lil-Nina**-88, **Conti Liban**-83, **Cremon**-75, lets the smaller **Marek** (ATG, 1999grt/83), ex **Elly Bojen**-95, overtake her shortly after leaving the locks on 12 September 2003. This is a common practice when one ship has to wait for oncoming traffic while others are allowed to proceed. In this case this is due to the former's deep draught. The village in the background is Holtenau after which the locks at this end of the canal are named. The **Debora** was built at Rendsburg by Werft Nobiskrug while **Marek** was built by Martin Jansen Schiffswerft in Leer. She belongs to the large fleet of Reederei Erwin Strahlmann.

Ebenfalls von der östlichen Holtenauer Hochbrücke bietet sich diese typische Szene. Am 12. September 2003 lässt die **Debora** (NIS, 2331 BRZ/65), ex **Porrino**-90, **Lil-Nina**-88, **Conti Liban**-83, **Cremon**-75, die kleinere **Marek** (ATG, 1999 BRZ/83), ex **Elly Bojen**-95, passieren, da Erstere wegen ihres Tiefgangs auf einen Entgegenkommer warten muss. Im Hintergrund ist Kiel-Holtenau zu erkennen, Namensgeber dieses Kanalendes. Beide Schiffe sind mit Schleswig-Holstein eng verbunden. Die **Debora** ist eines der zahlreichen am Kanal gebauten Schiffe. Sie entstand bei der Werft Nobiskrug in Rendsburg. **Marek** wurde zwar im ostfriesischen Leer bei der Martin Jansen Schiffswerft erbaut, gehört jedoch zu der großen Flotte des Reeders Erwin Strahlmann aus Marne in Dithmarschen.

(Oliver Sesemann)

When coastal shipping was not so much influenced by today's logistics chains with their tight schedules, coasters quite frequently used the moorings of the Binnenhafen siding directly in front of the locks at Kiel to stay overnight. Nowadays, it has become a rare sight to see a coaster moored here and therefore it certainly was unusual to see the *Ingelore* (DEU, 524gt/60), ex *Krautsand*-97, *Henriette II*-78, *Krautsand*-76, *Axel*-76, berthed for a number of days in early October 1998. Built at Sander Scheepsbouw shipyard in Delfzijl, she starred in the German TV series "Kümo Henriette" (*Coaster Henriette*) during her northern European years. In 2001 the coaster was sold to Caribbean interests and renamed *Eclair Express Cargo*, becoming *Debbie One* in 2002 and later *Isabella III*.

Vor der Übernahme durch moderne Logistiklösungen, als es in der Küstenschifffahrt noch etwas gemächlicher zuging, dienten die Dalben im Binnenhafen des öfteren als Nachtruheplätze für kleine Schiffe. Heute, in Zeiten straffer Fahrpläne, kommt dies entsprechend selten vor. So war es in der Tat außergewöhnlich, als Anfang Oktober 1998 die *Ingelore* (DEU, 524 BRZ/60), ex *Krautsand*-97, *Henriette II*-78, *Krautsand*-76, *Axel*-76, für einige Tage hier festmachte. Das bei Sander Scheepsbouw in Delfzijl erbaute Schiff wurde zuvor durch seine Hauptrolle in der Fernsehserie „Kümo Henriette" bekannt. Im Jahre 2001 wurde das Kümo in die Karibik verkauft und trug seitdem die Namen *Eclair Express Cargo*, wurde *Debbie One* in 2002 und später *Isabella III*.

(Oliver Sesemann)

A small passenger ferry, **Adler I** (DEU, 49gt), crosses the canal about 300 metres west of the locks at Holtenau. Again, this is a free ferry. It is ideal for anyone wishing to have a close-up view of passing shipping, but the small waiting area is also popular for onlookers. An added virtue is that a bus service terminates here, handy for anyone using public transport. The ferry passes close under the stern of the **Eros** (DEU, 1212gt/86), built at the canalside yard of Kröger- Werft, which is approaching the locks on 1 August 1991 heading for Turku from Esbjerg.

Am östlichen Ende der Weiche Binnenhafen, direkt vor den Schleusenleitwerken, kreuzt die kleine Personenfähre **Adler I** (DEU, 49 BRZ) zwischen den Stadtteilen Wik und Holtenau den Kanal. Sie und die Anlegestellen sind beliebte Ausflugsziele, besonders im Sommer. Am 1. August 1991 umrundet **Adler I** hier das Heck der **Eros** (DEU, 1212 BRZ/86), die am Kanal bei der Kröger-Werft in Schacht-Audorf entstand. Der Frachter befindet sich auf dem Weg von Esbjerg nach Turku.

(Bernard McCall)

We have arrived at the Baltic locks of the canal at Kiel-Holtenau. Like in Brunsbüttel, a new pair of locks was added during the waterway's first expansion between 1907 and 1914. Entering the southern chamber from the Kieler Förde fjord on 28 February 1999 is the attractive *Hanne Christine* (NIS, 2970gt/84), ex *Caribbean Breeze*-97, *Grimsnis*-93, *Blue Caribe Carrier*-93, *Grimsnis*-91, *Ville du Mistral*-85, *Grimsnis*-84. As the array of former names suggests, she had been chartered many times and indeed her powerful crane makes her a versatile vessel. *Hanne Christine* is yet another ship built by the Kröger-Werft at Schacht-Audorf on the canal. She is employed mainly on routes linking German and Norwegian ports.

Nun sind wir am östlichen Ende des NOK angekommen, den Holtenauer Schleusen in Kiel. Genau wie in Brunsbüttel wurden auch hier während der ersten Erweiterungsphase zwischen 1907 und 1914 zwei größere Schleusen hinzugefügt. Am 28. Februar 1999 läuft die *Hanne Christine* (NIS, 2970 BRZ/84), ex *Caribbean Breeze*-97, *Grimsnis*-93, *Blue Caribe Carrier*-93, *Grimsnis*-91, *Ville du Mistral*-85, *Grimsnis*-84 von See her die Südkammer dieser neuen Schleusen an. Wie die Exnamensliste vermuten lässt, war das Schiff bereits mehrfach verchartert worden; ihr großer Bordkran macht die *Hanne Christine* in der Tat zu einem sehr flexiblen Schiff. Sie ist ein weiteres bei Kröger in Schacht-Audorf entstandenes Exemplar und heute hauptsächlich zwischen Deutschland und Norwegen im Einsatz.

(Oliver Sesemann)

Until the IMO put thier new safety regulations into force in 2004, there was a viewing area on the southern side of the locks at Holtenau and this provides a fine general view although there are various obstructions which prevent unhindered photographs of ships. On 1 August 1991, the Sietas-built **Bianca** (CYP, 1934gt/72), ex **Atria**-86, enters the lock. She was on passage from Rotterdam to the Swedish port of Skelleftehamn. After being sold to Finnish owners in 2000, she was renamed **Cindy** but now has reverted to **Bianca** although still under the Finnish flag.

Bevor die internationalen Vorgaben der IMO zur Sicherheit in Hafenbereichen im Jahre 2004 verschäft wurden, gab es auf der Südseite der neuen Holtenauer Schleusen eine ausgezeichnete Aussichtsplattform für das interessierte Publikum. Einen Eindruck des Ausblicks ermöglicht diese Ansicht des Kümos **Bianca** (CYP, 1934 BRZ/72), ex **Atria**-86, das hier am 1. August 1991 von Rotterdam kommend einschleust. Es war auf dem Weg nach Skelleftehamn in Schweden. Im Jahre 2000 wurde das Schiff von finnischen Eignern in **Cindy** umbenannt, bekam jedoch später wieder den Namen **Bianca**.

(Bernard McCall)

On passage in ballast to St Petersburg, the **Slavyanka** (RUS, 2426gt/82), ex **Omskiy 110**-93, makes fast in the northern lock of the Neue Schleusen on 21 July 1995. Like many other Russian sea/river ships, she was built at the Santierul Naval shipyard in Oltenita.

Ein weiteres Exemplar der verschiedenen russischen Fluss-/Seeschiffe, die so regelmäßig auf dem Nord-Ostsee-Kanal zu sehen sind, ist die **Slavyanka** (RUS, 2426 BRZ/82), ex **Omskiy 110**-93, gebaut von der Werft Santierul Naval in Oltenita. Dieses Bild zeigt das Schiff am 21. Juli 1995 auf einer Ballastreise nach St. Petersburg beim Festmachen in der „Neuen Nord".

(Dominic McCall)

A crewman's view of the southern lock of the Neue Schleusen looking west on 27 May 1997. The *Magnus E* (ATG, 2768gt/83), ex *Veerhaven*-91, *Magnolia*-90, has just entered the lock when heading for Bremen from Liepaja. The ship was built at the Martin Jansen yard in Leer. In 1998, she was renamed *Dever* before becoming *Magnolia* again in 2001.

Die Perspektive eines Seemanns auf die Neue Nordschleuse am 27. Mai 1997: Der vorauslaufende Stammkunde *Magnus E* (ATG, 2768 BRZ/83), ex *Veerhaven*-91, *Magnolia*-90 ist gerade in die Kammer eingelaufen um nach der Schleusung seine Reise von Liepaja nach Bremen fortzusetzen. Das Schiff wurde auf der Martin Jansen Werft im ostfriesischen Leer gebaut und fuhr seit dem Zeitpunkt der Aufnahme noch als *Dever*, bevor es seinen aktuellen Namen - seinen Baunamen - *Magnolia* erhielt.

(Bernard McCall)

Having seen Wagenborg's *Osteborg* leaving the canal at Brunsbüttel on page 4, this is the *Oosterscheldeborg* (NLD, 3164gt/02) entering the new south lock at Kiel, about to leave the canal after her maiden passage on a sunny 9 September 2002. She has just been delivered by Peters Scheepswerf of Kampen, Netherlands. Her fleetmate *MSC Poland* (NLD, 6540gt/00), ex *Mississippiborg*-00, is leaving the north lock en route from the Baltic with containers for her charterers, Mediterranean Shipping Company.

Zu Beginn verließ die *Osteborg* den Kanal in Brunsbüttel (s. S. 4), hier ist es die *Oosterscheldeborg* (NLD, 3164 BRZ/02), die am sonnigen 9. September 2002 in die neue Südkammer der Holtenauer Schleusen einläuft, um nach ihrer ersten Passage den NOK in Richtung Ostsee zu verlassen. Sie ist soeben von der Peters-Werft im niederländischen Kampen abgeliefert worden. Ein weiteres Wagenborg-Schiff, die *MSC Poland* (NLD, 6540 BRZ/00), ex *Mississippiborg*-00, verlässt derweil westwärts die neue Nordschleuse mit einer Ladung Container für seinen Charterer, die Mediterranean Shipping Company.

(Oliver Sesemann)

Entering the southern lock of the Neue Schleusen from the Kieler Förde on 4 April 1999 is the *Verena* (NLD, 1769gt/77), ex *Mathilde*-77, built at the "Voorwaarts" shipyard in Hoogezand. The shop is very popular with seamen who call there whilst their ship is in the lock. Not only does it sell duty-free goods but it also provides essentials such as charts. When the photo was taken on 4 April 1999, this typical Dutch coaster sailed for Wijnne & Barends Cargadoors- en agentuurskantoren BV. After her sale to Greece in 2002, the *Verena* left Northern Europe for the Mediterranean where she now sails as *Eleni K*.

Erfolgreich im internationalen Geschäft ist der Schleusenshop im Gebäude des Schleusenleitstandes auf der Mittelmauer der Neuen Schleusen. Seeleute von nah und fern decken sich hier mit Nötigem ein, was zollfreie Waren und Seekarten sein können. Kundschaft naht hier am 4. April 1999 an Bord der *Verena* (NLD, 1769 BRZ/77), ex *Mathilde*-77, ein typischer „Hollandbau" der Voorwaarts-Werft in Hoogezand. Damals für Wijnne & Barends Cargadoors- en agentuurskantoren BV fahrend, ist dieser ehemalige Stammkunde des Kanals im Jahre 2002 nach Griechenland verkauft, in *Eleni K* umbenannt und ins Mittelmeer verlegt worden.

(Bernard McCall)

Until very recently, the old locks at Holtenau were used for emergency and relief purposes or, during the summer months, for pleasure craft but since early 2005 they have been opened again for commercial traffic because of the increased traffic on the canal. Seen passing Holtenau marina on her approach to the old south lock from the Baltic Sea is the veteran Danish coaster **Monsunen** (DIS, 383gt/65), ex *Ota Riis*-72. This summer view dated early June 2003 shows the narrow confines of the old lock entrance with two of the many Tall Ships that flock to the Baltic at this time of year berthed right at the fairway. The ice-strengthened **Monsunen** was built at the Ørskovs Staalskibsvaerft I/S shipyard in Frederikshavn. She is a regular caller on the canal.

Die alten Holtenauer Schleusen dienten in der Folge lange Zeit jedoch nur als Ersatz sowie in den Sommermonaten als Sportbootschleusen. Wegen der rapide steigenden Verkehrszahlen wurden sie im Frühjahr 2005 jedoch wieder regulär für die Handelsschifffahrt geöffnet. Der dänische Veteran und Kanal-Stammkunde **Monsunen** (DIS, 383 BRZ/65), ex *Ota Riis*-72, läuft hier von See kommend im Sommer 2003 die Südkammer an. Diese Perspektive verdeutlicht die Enge der Einfahrt direkt am Holtenauer Sportboothafen in besonderer Weise: Zwei der Großsegler, die in der Sommersaison in Scharen nach Kiel strömen, liegen direkt am Fahrwasser. **Monsunen** wurde von der Ørskovs Staalskibsvaerft I/S in Frederikshavn als eisverstärkter coaster erbaut und ist somit prädestiniert für den winterlichen Ostseeverkehr.

(Oliver Sesemann)

Inside the old north lock now, this undated view from the 1970s certainly shows a busy day. The front left ship is **Gunda-Gisela** (DEU, 1909), ex **Adele Hagenah**-65, **Peter Ahrens**-59, **Albert Friesecke**-58, built as **Wilhelm**- at the Frerichs shipyard of Einswarden. Following a sale in 1978, the veteran was scrapped in Vigo in 1981 as **Azores**. The front right coaster is the Voorwarts Hijlkema-built **Clarissa** (NLD, 496gt/67), later sold several times and renamed **Woolacombe**, **Josiane** and again **Woolacombe**. Today she sails as **Lady Fazeela**. The **Marlow** (DDR, 466gt/71), back left, was built at Elbewerft Boizenburg and sailed for Deutsche Seereederei (the East German state shipping company) until sold and renamed **Maria** before becoming the Australian **Northern Express** in 2003. Beside her is an unidentified coaster, probably of Danish origin. The ro/ro ship **Algol** (DEU, 2720gt/72) is entering the old south lock. This vessel was built by Kröger-Werft shipyard and today sails as **Cedar Car**.

Dieses undatierte Foto aus den 1970er Jahren zeigt eine unzweifelhaft geschäftige alte Nordkammer. Das Schiff vorn links ist die bei Frerichs in Einswarden als **Wilhelm** gebaute **Gunda-Gisela** (DEU, 1909), ex **Adele Hagenah**-65, **Peter Ahrens**-59, **Albert Friesecke**-58. Zwischen ihrem Verkauf 1978 und ihrer Verschrottung 1981 in Vigo fuhr sie noch als **Azores**. Neben ihr liegt die **Clarissa** (NLD, 496 BRZ/67), gebaut bei Voorwarts Hijlkema. Dieses Schiff wurde später noch in **Woolacombe**, **Josiane** und wieder **Woolacombe** umbenannt und fährt heute als **Lady Fazeela**. Die in Boizenburg entstandene **Marlow** (DDR, 466 BRZ/71), hinten links, fährt hier für die Deutsche Seereederei in Rostock. Sie wurde später verkauft und in **Maria** umbenannt. Heute führt das Schiff als **Northern Express** die australische Flagge. Neben ihr liegt ein nicht identifiziertes, wahrscheinlich dänisches Kümo. In die Südkammer läuft gerade die bei Kröger gebaute **Algol** (DEU, 2720 BRZ/72) ein, die heute als **Cedar Car** unterwegs ist.

(Uwe Fischer)

Tiessenkai quay in Kiel-Holtenau is situated just outside the lock area but still within the official limits of the Kiel Canal as part of which it was constructed. It serves as a shelter berth for small vessels up to 5 metres draught. It features many historic buildings among which is the lighthouse (1895), marking the canal's entrance. The coaster seen at this beautiful spot on 17 January 2000 is the Danish "Caroliner" *Caroline Samsø* (DNK, 159gt/59), ex *Jane*-94, *Janto*-65. The ship was preparing to sail back to Denmark, having delivered a load of grain to Nordhafen grain terminal (s.a.), together with sister ship *Samka*, from which the photo was taken. Both ships are privately preserved and earn their money by commercial voyages and as floating exhibition centres.

Der Tiessenkai liegt zwar außerhalb der Schleusen, aber noch innerhalb der Kilometerzählung des NOK. Er entstand im Zuge des Kanalbaus und dient als Schutzhafen für Kümos bis zu einem Tiefgang von ungefähr fünf Metern. Viele alte Gebäude zieren den schönen Kai, gekrönt durch den Holtenauer Leuchtturm (1895), eines der Einfahrtszeichen der Wasserstraße. Das Kümo auf diesem Bild vom 17. Januar 2000 ist der dänische „Caroliner" *Caroline Samsø* (DNK, 159 BRZ/59), ex *Jane*-94, *Janto*-65. Zusammen mit dem Schwesterschiff *Samka*, von dem aus das Foto entstand, hatte der kleine Frachter zuvor Getreide zum Nordhafen gebracht und bereitet sich hier auf die Rückfahrt vor. Beide Schiffe werden von privat als Museumsschiffe erhalten und verdienen sich mit solchen Fahrten sowie als schwimmende Austellungsräume ihren Unterhalt

(Oliver Sesemann)

Arriving at the Tiessenkai quay to take on stores on 14 July 1999 is the **Andries** (NLD, 648gt/72), ex **Thalassa**-83, **Douwe-S**-81, **Trinitas**-77. This coaster was built at the van Goor shipyard in Monnickendam. In 2001, she was sold to a Belgian owner by whom she was renamed **Metatron**. Since then she has sailed only on inland waterways.

Am 14. Juli 1999 läuft die **Andries** (NLD, 648 BRZ/72), ex **Thalassa**-83, **Douwe-S**-81, **Trinitas**-77, den Tiessenkai an, um bei Hermann Tiessen Proviant zu übernehmen. Dieses Kümo wurde von der van Goor-Werft im niederländischen Monnickendam erbaut. Nachdem es im Jahre 2001 nach Belgien verkauft und von den neuen Eignern in **Metatron** umbenannt wurde, fuhr das Schiff nur noch auf europäischen Binnenwasserstraßen.

(Dominic McCall)

Leaving the locks at Kiel and heading for the Baltic on a sunny 26 June 2003 is the **Tone** (FRO, 1331gt/70), ex **Conny T**-85, **Traffic**-81, **Dynacontainer III**-72, launched as **Wally Bos**. The ship's stone handling gear is typical of her kind, enabling her to trade in the aggregates trades of northern Europe which include many a tiny port or wharf too small or remote to provide land-based equipment. Tiessenkai can be seen in the background of this view. The large building prominent in this picture is a preserved warehouse built in 1783/84 when the Eiderkanal, the predecessor of today's Kiel Canal, was constructed. The **Tone** was built at the "De Dageraad" yard of J Boot in Woubrugge.

Am 26. Juni 2003 verlässt die **Tone** (FRO, 1331 BRZ/70), ex **Conny T**-85, **Traffic**-81, **Dynacontainer III**-72, vom Stapel als **Wally Bos**, die Holtenauer Schleusen gen Ostsee. Der aufgesetzte Bagger ist das dient als typisches Ladegeschirr vieler Schiffe, die in Nordeuropa Steine und andere Baumaterialien transportieren. Dieser Handel führt die Schiffe oftmals in kleine Häfen, teilweise schlichte Piers, die keine eigene Verlademöglichkeit haben. Im Hintergrund ist der Tiessenkai mit dem historischen Kanalpackhaus zu sehen, das 1783/84 im Zuge des Eiderkanal-Baus errichtet wurde und in Tönning eine Schwester hat.

(Oliver Sesemann)

Yet another coaster built at the Kröger-Werft yard is the attractive **San Remo** (MLT, 1283gt/65), ex **Saxen**-89. This ship is approaching the lock entrance area between Tiessenkai and Scheerhafen on a sunny 25 March 2003. In the background the emergency tug **Bülk** (left) and Lindenau shipyard's facilities (centre) can be seen.

Ein weiteres Produkt der Kröger-Werft ist die attraktive **San Remo** (MLT, 1283 BRZ/65), ex **Saxen**-89, die hier am sonnigen 25. März 2003 den Schleusenvorhafen zwischen Tiessenkai und Scheermole passiert. Im Hintergrund sind der Schlepper **Bülk** (links) und die Lindenau-Werft zu sehen.

(Oliver Sesemann)

Crossing the line between Scheermole (right) and Holtenau (background) lighthouses on 25 March 2003 is the chemical tanker **Orahope** (DIS, 2631gt/02). Here, the canal ends at the 98.637 kilometre point. The ship belongs to the Danish Rederiet M H Simonsen ApS, of Svendborg, and was built in Turkey by the Gemyat shipyard.

Am 25. März 2003 überquert der Chemietanker **Orahope** (DIS, 2631 BRZ/02) die 98,637 km-Linie, das offizielle Ende des Kanals, zwischen den Leuchttürmen Nordmole (Vordergrund) und Holtenau (Hintergrund). Das Schiff wurde von der türkischen Gemyat-Werft im Auftrag für die dänische Rederiet M. H. Simonsen ApS mit Sitz in Svendborg gebaut.

(Oliver Sesemann)